VEGETABLE GARDENING

A Beginner's Guide to Cultivating Your Own Vegetable Garden

By Luke Smith

VEGETABLE GARDENING

© Copyright 2020 - All rights reserved.

The content contained within this book may not be reproduced, duplicated or transmitted without direct written permission from the author or the publisher.

Under no circumstances will any blame or legal responsibility be held against the publisher, or author, for any damages, reparation, or monetary loss due to the information contained within this book. Either directly or indirectly.

Legal Notice:

This book is copyright protected. This book is only for personal use. You cannot amend, distribute, sell, use, quote or paraphrase any part, or the content within this book, without the consent of the author or publisher.

Disclaimer Notice:

Please note the information contained within this document is for educational and entertainment purposes only. All effort has been executed to present accurate, up to date, and reliable, complete information. No warranties of any kind are declared or implied. Readers acknowledge that the author is not engaging in the rendering of legal, financial, medical or professional advice. The content within this book has been derived from various sources. Please consult a licensed professional before attempting any techniques outlined

VEGETABLE GARDENING

in this book.

By reading this document, the reader agrees that under no circumstances is the author responsible for any losses, direct or indirect, which are incurred as a result of the use of information contained within this document, including, but not limited to, — errors, omissions, or inaccuracies.

VEGETABLE GARDENING

Table of Contents

Introduction v

Chapter One - Why Start A Vegetable Garden? 1

Chapter Two - Planning Your Vegetable Garden 18

Chapter Three - How To Plant Your Vegetables 43

Chapter Four - Maintaining Your Garden 74

Chapter Five - Harvesting And Preserving 100

Chapter Six - Pest Control And Disease Prevention 129

Final Words 140

INTRODUCTION

Vegetable gardening is one of our species's oldest jobs. Humans first started exploring and practicing agriculture around 9500 BCE, or more than 11,000 years ago. It was this discovery, that not only does the ground produce food, but we are also able to control that production, which allowed us to start forming villages, towns and eventually cities.

Agriculture brought many advances. Medicines could be grown; ancient Egyptians began to use plants like aloe vera as medicines. Agriculture also paved the way for us to start producing textiles like cotton or hemp. But none of these discoveries hold a candle to vegetable gardening. Before the discovery of agriculture, it wasn't uncommon for tribes of humans to be starved throughout the winter; great swaths of the population were often wiped out due to lack of food. Being able to control the production of food allowed us to make enough food to store throughout the winter and avoid starvation. It absolutely changed the future of mankind; we went from being primitive animals to inventing the written word so that these practices could pass down from generation to generation.

The switch into agricultural practices created a new way of living. For centuries to come, being a farmer would be seen as a noble tradition. Often discriminated against due to the laws of the ruling class, these hardworking individuals kept the kingdoms and villages supplied with food. Despite all the hardships, vegetable farmers were a necessary part of the human equation.

It wasn't until the emergence of nowadays' modern man that vegetable gardening and farming started to get a bad rap. With all the new technologies that are invented everyday and the fact that you can go to the grocery store and find any vegetable you want, the concept of vegetable gardener and farmer have begun to seem less appealing to the average person. Now, instead of learning how to garden, young adults are heading off for an education in law or business. Others would look towards fame and fortune, either succeeding or burning out along the way.

As the twentieth century came to an end, it seemed as if vegetable gardening as a career, hobby, or even an interest was fading away, just another feature of the distant past that no longer concerned mankind as it moved into the future. When you can order your food online and chemical treatments produce vegetables twice the size they were in the past, it seemed clear that getting your hands dirty in the soil was no longer needed.

But the twenty-first century has seen this reversed. As man has created more technology and automated more and more processes, there has been a fatigue that has cropped up. People have started to get tired of all of the chemicals being pumped into their food; they are no longer as appealing as they once were. There has been a movement towards embracing green or environmentally sound practices, as well as a push towards organic foods that are free of harmful chemicals.

The twenty-first century man has found that returning to the soil is a peaceful experience. There is a sense of pride in growing your own food, a feeling of doing something that matters and getting back to the roots of what it means to be a human, by taking part in and sharing an experience that has connected human beings together for more than four hundred generations.

With this book, you will learn how you, too, can feel this sense of peace, pride and connection to the world around you by growing your own vegetable garden. In chapter one you will learn the many positive reasons to start a vegetable garden of your own. Chapter two will help you plan your garden and consider the kinds of vegetables you will be able to grow. Chapter three will teach you all about how to plant those vegetables from seeding to soiling. Chapter four will explore the steps we take to maintain that garden so it gets plenty of the necessary nutrients to grow large, healthy harvests. Those harvests will be our focus in chapter five, along with how to preserve your newly harvested vegetables. Finally, chapter six will teach you all about the various pests and diseases which you will find yourself fighting;

the preventative steps in the chapter will help you avoid those fights as long as possible. Some final thoughts on where to go next to learn further information and continue your journey from beginner to expert are also included in this chapter.

CHAPTER ONE

WHY START A VEGETABLE GARDEN?

If you are still reading this book, then you must already be considering starting your own vegetable garden. This consideration was probably spawned by one of the reasons that we'll be looking at in this chapter. I feel comfortable making this assumption because, as you will see, there are a ton of reasons why somebody would want to start a vegetable garden, which range from finances to health and from the environmental impact to the mental benefits.

While the information in this chapter won't be able to tell you if vegetable gardening is a good fit for you or not, it will give you enough reasons to make the initial investment and give vegetable gardening a try. With all of these benefits in mind, the earlier challenges faced when growing your own vegetables won't seem as difficult because you will be able to clearly see the reward.

It's Organic (and Tastier!)

One of the big changes in the last few years has been the strong push towards organically grown vegetables. The use of chemicals in order to fertilize or treat crops for pest control makes perfect sense when you consider vegetable farming as an industry. The goal of any business is to ultimately make money. A farming business may have a mission statement about the quality of their food or the happiness that it brings to the table, but at the end of the day that business doesn't exist without making money. Chemicals, which quickly kill off pests, and fertilizers, which produce larger than average vegetables allow for larger yields at a lower cost.

VEGETABLE GARDENING

Considering that these vegetables then need to be shipped around the country to various stores, you can see why this business model works.

The problem is that those same chemicals are not very healthy for humans to eat. Our bodies weren't designed to be pumped full of strange chemicals. They did evolve to eat vegetables and other naturally grown products. Growing your vegetables with an organic approach removes these harmful chemicals from the equation so that you don't find yourself consuming poison or carcinogenic toxins. This makes growing your own vegetables a healthy choice, though it is far from the only reason it is healthier.

But let's say that you aren't concerned about chemicals in your food. You've been eating store-bought vegetables your whole life and you've never had any health problems. Why should you care about going organic? If you don't care about health then you should go organic because it tastes better. Studies show that organically grown foods are rated as tastier when subjects perform taste tests between organically and chemically grown vegetables. Scientists are still looking to explain whether this is due to biological or psychological reasons. So far, the results suggest that it is both. But regardless of the reason, people swear that organic foods taste better. So if you don't care about your health, care about your taste buds and give organic vegetable gardening a try.

VEGETABLE GARDENING

It's Cheaper

If you want to buy your own vegetables then you have two options. The most commonly chosen way to get vegetables is to walk or drive down to the nearest grocery store and see what is in stock. The quality of the vegetables in a grocery store can be great but more often than not they are simply average or even unappealing. Regardless of the quality, you still end up paying the same price all the same.

The other way that people buy vegetables is to head to the local farmer's market and find a seller. These are often higher quality vegetables, but they can range in price to be both less or more than grocery store bought vegetables, as the price is determined by the individual seller.

In the first example, the price of vegetables needs to be enough so that the grocery store makes a profit on them. This means that they need to cover the cost of storage and transportation, as well as the price they were purchased at in the first place. The farmer's market price needs to also cover enough for the table at the market, the price of getting the vegetables to the market and the cost of growing them in the first place.

This is a lot of money that is being exchanged for services rather than the vegetables themselves. The best way to lower the cost of the vegetables in your diet is to grow them yourself. You will need to invest a little money up front and throughout the growing process but this investment will pay for itself quickly as your grocery bill shrinks. The most cost effective way to have fresh vegetables is to cut out all the middlemen and grow your own.

But while we're on the topic of money…

Make Money With a Vegetable Garden

We just got done talking about saving money by avoiding the farmer's market, but the flipside to that particular benefit is the fact that you could be the one selling vegetables there. If you have your own garden then you can harvest your crops, take what you need for yourself and sell the rest locally. Many gardeners even maintain a garden for themselves and one for crops they are planning to sell.

If you are growing vegetables in your garden anyway, then adding a couple more with the intent to sell what they produce can be a great way to earn back your initial investment. If you switch to eating your own vegetables rather than buying them, you are going to save money on the grocery bill, but the initial investment will not be repaid in the strictest definition. If you take those same vegetables and sell them, you can earn back that investment with extra to cover the interest.

Keep in mind that the initial investment to start a vegetable garden isn't very high anyway, so it can quickly turn a profit if that is your intention. Outdoor gardens will only be able to make money on a seasonal basis but indoor vegetable gardeners can keep growing vegetables throughout the year. We are going to focus on outdoor gardening here, but indoor growing is worth researching if you intend to use your vegetable gardening skills to earn money.

You Eat Healthier and More Creatively When You Have a Vegetable Garden

The lack of harmful chemicals was only one of the reasons that having your own vegetable garden is a healthy choice. When they start growing their own vegetables, most beginners are surprised at how much they are able to harvest. These nutritious plants end up in all sorts of different meals, if for no other reason than the fact that they need to be used (or preserved) before they can go bad. To boot, these vegetables are free if you already have the supplies, whereas store bought vegetables cost you money. Due to cost, most people purchase smaller quantities of vegetables compared to what a vegetable garden can yield in a good season.

Let's say you are a fan of carrots, so you purchase them a lot. Chances are you get one or two bags of them in your fridge at any given time. You might consider buying more of them when they are on sale, but then many people find they don't go through them fast enough to get through the bags before the carrots go bad. Since there are only so many carrots in the house, it is always an easier choice to cook them up in a way that is familiar and safe. However, when you have tons of them from a good harvest, you will find yourself getting creative with your meals. There are thousands of new recipes to be found on the internet every day and it is much less riskier to ruin a few carrots when you have tons, unlike when you buy them from the store.

VEGETABLE GARDENING

This level of creativity is something that you will often hear new gardeners talking about after their first good yield. People don't really consider this to be one of the benefits from gardening because it seems detached from the physical work of planting seeds and getting your hands dirty in the soil. But having more vegetables around the house leads to healthier meals with more variety and experimentation. You might just discover your new favorite recipe this way.

It's Better for the Environment

While we were discussing the price of store-bought veggies, we saw that there are a ton of middle men who need to get paid in order for chemically grown vegetables to make their way onto the shelves of your local grocery store. This process actually has two costs required to keep it functioning. The first is the money that is necessary for everyone along this production line to be paid. This is the cost that is reflected in what you pay at the till and in your weekly budget. The second cost is the environmental cost. This cost can't be budgeted as easily, but it can be seen by turning on the news or reading about our current climate crisis. Growing your own vegetables helps you to cut not just the first cost but both of them.

One environmental cost that is a direct result of modern farming practices is the amount of chemicals that are poisoning the environment. Most of the chemicals used on your food aren't poison in a direct manner. That is, you can eat traces of them without getting sick (though there are exceptions to this). But these chemicals are the most harmful to the environment itself; runoff from fields affects the wildlife in the surrounding areas and seeps into nearby bodies of water. Unfortunately, starting your own vegetable garden is not going to have a strong impact on this. This is the result of large scale operations. But switching from store-bought produce to veggies you've produced yourself will keep you from funneling more money into these harmful practices. Less money being funnelled into environmentally-abusive hands is always a good thing.

Starting your own vegetable garden is more impactful in reducing the amount of fossil fuels that are burnt as part of your eating. When you go to the grocery store and purchase vegetables, you are also paying for the gas that was required to move that vegetable across the country. By growing your own vegetables, you create food without having to burn fossil fuels, which reduces your carbon footprint. If you sell those vegetables locally, then you are able to reduce the amount of vegetables that need to be shipped into your local area, which means that you are also helping to reduce the carbon footprint of your community this way.

VEGETABLE GARDENING

If you don't care about the environment as much, then at least consider the fact that the less fossil fuels being burned, the less money you are spending to keep you and your family fed. It would have taken a trip to the grocery store to get your vegetables but since you have a crop of your own you don't need to waste the time or the gas needed to drive there. All it takes is your two hands and legs and a couple minutes to go grab something from out of the garden.

Growing Your Own Vegetables is Great Exercise

There is nothing more refreshing than a little bit of exercise after a long day of work. It seems like a contradiction to push yourself when you are tired but studies show it leaves you healthier and feeling more energized. Some people head to the gym to lift weights after work, others go for a nice long jog. One way that thousands of people across the world get their exercise is through working in their gardens. Despite often being down on your hands and knees, vegetable gardening is a great way to get exercise and this is just another of the many ways that starting a vegetable garden is an investment in your health.

Soil needs to be mixed and moved around the yard. You need to get down to the plants level and then up to your feet again. It gets you outdoors in the natural sunlight, which is a natural antidepressant, and the fresh air, which makes the lungs happy. These elements release endorphins in your brain which make you feel happier, while the exercise keeps the body healthy and working well. So instead of paying for a monthly gym pass, you can get your exercise while growing a crop that will pay you instead.

If you have a weak disposition, then vegetable gardening can be a good way to get exercise at a slower pace than other approaches. Those with strong bodies and active lifestyles are going to receive lesser benefits in this regard, but getting out of the house and enjoying the fresh air is great for the mind, body, and soul.

Grow a Variety of Foods

Most vegetable gardens are full of staples; lettuce and carrots, potatoes and tomatoes, pumpkins and peppers are common. You are free to grow one of these or all of them as you see fit, and this offers plenty of variety. It doesn't need to be carrots for dinner every night, your options are only limited by what you decide to grow.

Of course, you are going to need to consider the climate of your local area to determine what you can or can't grow. If you want to grow a plant that needs high humidity, but you live in a dry area, then you aren't going to be able to easily provide the environment necessary to grow this plant. Indoor gardeners can control their growing environment and so have no problem with this but outdoor vegetable gardeners are going to need to consider their resources before planting any new seeds.

This isn't as limiting as it might seem. The fact of the matter is that there are thousands of possibilities for what you can grow in your vegetable garden. Not only are there going to be all sorts of vegetables that will work perfectly, but also this number grows exponentially when you take into account the many subspecies there are. For example, tomatoes can be fist sized or you can choose to grow cherry tomatoes instead.

If you are looking to make money growing vegetables, then take a trip to your local farmer market and see what people are growing already. Once you know what is available, pay attention to what is missing. If someone is selling tomatoes, are they also selling cherry tomatoes? With the amount of variety there is when it comes to growing your own vegetables, you can fill a niche that isn't being serviced or you can grow your favorite vegetables that the stores don't seem to carry often.

Remember that just because we will be looking at certain vegetables in this book, it doesn't mean that you have to grow any of them. Grow whatever your taste buds (or wallet) desires, just remember to research the plant beforehand to ensure it thrives in your climate.

Vegetable Gardening Fosters a Sense of Pride and Connection

There is something amazing about planting a tiny seed and watching it grow into a full sized (and delicious) vegetable, knowing that the only reason that happened was because of your skill and effort. People get into gardening for the same reason they get into arts or crafts. The sense of pride that comes from creating something refined and useful out of raw materials has driven people towards these fields for centuries. The only difference between gardening and carpentry is that the plants are alive and you must think of them as such.

When you forget that a plant is a living being, you lose that nurturing touch that is necessary to keep your plants healthy and happy. Plants have certain requirements and a language of physical responses to indicate when one of those requirements isn't being met. When you pay attention to your plants and respond to the messages they give you, the plants reward you in turn with larger and more delicious vegetables. In this way, working with your plants becomes a conversation that is mutually beneficial and richly rewarding.

VEGETABLE GARDENING

Learning to listen to the plants in your garden gives you a much deeper sense of connection to the environment and the world around you. You can see the way that plants speak to us about their needs; this connection often brings a lot of compassion into a gardener's world. It also makes it easier for some gardeners to share that compassion with other animals and their fellow man. If everyone stopped to learn this knowledge and experience, this connection to nature and the world would be a better place. If nothing else, everybody would be able to take pride in knowing how to grow their own food.

VEGETABLE GARDENING

Chapter Summary

- There are many reasons why you should be growing your own vegetables, from health to money and environmental concerns.

- Growing your own vegetables is a natural process that doesn't use harmful chemicals. It just so happens that studies show that organic vegetables taste better, as well, so this is a reason that is healthy for your body and rewarding for your taste buds.

- It costs money to purchase fresh vegetables from the grocery store or farmer's markets every week. While it costs a little bit of money to start your own garden, you can take that same investment and use it to grow crops and crops of your own delicious veggies.

- If you have extra vegetables left over after a harvest, then you can sell them at your local farmer's market. You could even grow vegetables just to be able to sell them and earn your money back. Many gardeners do both, grow to sell and to enjoy.

- Having access to plenty of fresh garden veggies will keep you making healthy choices and eating lots of nutrition goodness. It also has a tendency to push gardeners into getting experimental with

VEGETABLE GARDENING

how they cook up their vegetables and trying new dishes.

- Growing your own vegetables eliminates the need for fossil fuels to be burned since you don't need to transport anything. You stop putting money into the hands of companies that are damaging the environment and this helps lessen your carbon footprint.

- Gardening is exercise. There is soil to move, lots of getting up from being on your knees and tons of yanking out harmful weeds. All of this helps get endorphins pumping through your body to help you feel good and stay in shape.

- When you have your own vegetable garden you can grow whatever you like. You can grow vegetables that are not sold in your local grocery store. There are tons and tons of different species and subspecies of veggies just waiting for you to start planting them.

- Working in a vegetable garden teaches you how to listen to the plants and feel compassion for a living object that is different from yourself. This fosters a sense of connection to the world around you and compassion for the living creatures you are sharing it with.

In the next chapter you will learn how to plan your very own vegetable garden. It is important to keep in

VEGETABLE GARDENING

mind considerations of space, ease of access, amount of daylight and temperature (and more) when planning your garden. These variables change depending on what veggies you are looking to grow, so we'll explore these all in turn and see what some of the more popular crops need. This will give you everything you need to consider before you start planting.

CHAPTER TWO

PLANNING YOUR VEGETABLE GARDEN

Planning your vegetable garden might not sound like the funnest part of the process, and you'd be right to think so. At this stage you don't even get your hands dirty. There are considerations of space and logistics which need to be considered, and these can be pretty boring to figure out. But by planning your garden properly, you will be equipped with all the knowledge you need to have in order to understand exactly what conditions your plants are growing in. Just because it is boring, it doesn't mean it has to be hard. This chapter is split into two separate parts; all of this process will be covered in the first part.

The second part will be where the planning actually gets pretty fun. Once you understand the factors of the first half, it is time to start picking and choosing which vegetables you are going to grow. We'll highlight a handful of veggies during this part and cover some basic planning tips. By the end of this chapter, you'll know what seeds you are getting and where they'll be growing.

Deciding Where to Plant Your Garden

If we are going to be starting a vegetable garden, then the very first thing that we need to do is pick a location for our vegetable garden. It's easy enough to look out your window at your backyard and say you've got it figured out, but it really isn't that simple. In your backyard, there are dozens of places in which you could plant your garden depending on how you space it or position it, and also the size of your backyard. Each possibility is technically in your backyard but locations aren't all made the same. Some are better than others and some are downright unsuitable for gardening.

In this stage of your planning, you should take a moment to consider each of the following environmental attributes. Some of these you can tell just by looking at your yard but others will require a little bit of data gathering. These steps are included where necessary. You can get by with growing in a location that is a little less than ideal for some of these attributes, but spots which fail on multiple fronts are best avoided.

Elevation: This one can usually be done through eyesight alone. Looking at the space you are thinking about planting your vegetables, is it elevated? Is it on an incline? Is it at the bottom of an incline? Is it rather flat? Depending on which of these questions is the most accurate, you are going to have a unique relationship to watering your plants. Generalized advice on watering your plants assumes that they are in a flat space. Plants that are on an incline will act flat. Plants on the bottom of an incline are going to need less water. Those planted on an elevated surface will require more water than normal.

Sunlight: Plants need a certain amount of sunlight a day. Some species prefer this light to be direct, others prefer it to be indirect, in the shade. Some want as much sun as possible, while others need relatively little direct sunlight. If you are going to be growing vegetables, then you are going to need to know two things. You are going to need to research the species of plant to see how much sunlight it needs, and you are going to need to know how much sun your chosen space gets. Keep an eye on the space throughout a day and see how much time it is in the sun and in the shade. Finding this out will let you know which vegetables will do best in this particular space. If you are looking to plant some veggies that want a lot of sun and some that don't want much, then remember that you don't need to grow everything in the same bed. It is better to grow multiple beds than try to force a plant out of its comfort zone.

VEGETABLE GARDENING

Coverage: How much foliage or coverage from rain and wind does the space have? Are plants going to be safe from high winds where you plant them? Are they going to be able to get enough water when it rains or is the foliage going to misdirect it? Flipside, is the foliage going to help to prevent drier plants from drowning? Coverage isn't necessary when it comes to vegetable gardening but many gardeners have no choice but to work with it because of having trees in their backyards or limited space.

Security: How safe are your vegetables? Vegetable farming doesn't tend to bring out thieves the same way that cannabis or fruit farming does. Well, at least not human thieves. Vegetable farming does bring out mice, rabbits, deer and other herbivores. While seeing a deer eating your vegetables is a good sign (after all, it means they must be pretty tasty), it also means that you now have a half ruined crop. If there is easy access to your backyard or growing space then you should consider how you can add some security to prevent unwanted visitors. This can be as easy as adding a knee level plastic fence around the garden but if you can offer security in one direction (such as when growing next to a house) then you can save money by using less fencing and limiting critters from approaching.

Ease of Access: This is the one factor that causes the most problems, but new gardeners don't realize it until it is too late. When you are first planning out your garden, it is easy to forget about the fact that you are going to need to be able to maneuver through it. Maintaining your crops requires you to water each plant and inspect it for signs of problems. If you plant your crops in such a way that you can't get easy access to some of them, then you are going to end up neglecting those plants and they will reflect this in their yield. Most gardeners get a pack of vegetable seeds and then plant them too close together. When the plant you are growing is so tiny to begin with, it is easy to forget what size they are going to be growing to. This is the reason that crops are most often planted in rows. Try to keep size in mind and ensure that there is enough space for you not only to get at every plant but to be able to get down and inspect each one.

Ground or Container: The majority of this book is written under the assumption that you are growing your plants in the ground itself. That said, we will briefly address potting plants in chapter three. At this stage, it is important to note that, while there are some general differences between these two methods, there are also many similarities. Whether you are growing containers that are above ground or below ground, they tend to need to be watered more often than plants grown outside of a container. Beyond this main difference, they will still require as much sunlight, security and ease of access as any other garden bed you plant.

VEGETABLE GARDENING

Putting It All Together: Once you have considered each of these attributes of the space, you can decide if it will be a good fit for your plants or not, as determined by their needs. Figuring out each of these attributes will take time and make it a longer wait before you are ready to plant your vegetables, but it can save you from some nasty surprises that could lead to weak veggies and poor yield. A spot that looks perfect at first glance might not get enough sunlight or shade for the plants you were looking to put there. Knowing this ahead of time allows you to match your garden to the local conditions so you can have the most productive vegetable garden possible.

Planning the Vegetables in Your Garden

Now we're onto the fun part of planning. We can start to imagine what delicious veggies we are going to be eating in the near future. We will finish this chapter by looking at what it takes to grow carrots, peppers, tomatoes, and broccoli. Before we look at these specific examples it would serve well to take a moment to consider our location again.

As noted above, it is better to plant multiple garden beds for plants with different needs. You will know exactly how much space you have to work with and what conditions you are able to give your veggies. Use this to decide what to plant and which spot it should be in. You can grow anything you want, just research its needs ahead of time so that you know in which space to put it and how to keep it healthy. The following highlights will discuss aspects of environment, care, and maintenance, all of which will be discussed throughout the remainder of the book, so that you have the required knowledge to take care of any type of vegetable you desire.

How to Grow Carrots

Carrots are a beloved vegetable to humans and bunnies all over the world. These orange root vegetables like the colder weather around the start of the spring or the end of the fall where temperatures are around 75F during daytime and fifteen or twenty degrees colder during the night. While carrots enjoy the sun, they are one of the species that can get by just fine with some shade.

Carrots are planted in rows that are a couple feet apart from each other to allow each plant enough space to grow, as well as to allow gardeners access to each plant. Seeds themselves are planted inches apart throughout the row, and half an inch below the surface of the soil. The soil shouldn't have any large particles in it that can interfere with the roots. The soil itself should be loose enough to allow plenty of oxygen to the roots and quick draining. It is best to use a sandy mixture for this and avoid mineral-heavy soil, as this often leads to disfigured vegetables.

As seedlings begin to emerge, gardeners are required to thin out the rows so that there are a few inches between plants. It may feel weird to remove plants you worked hard to grow, but doing this allows the plants left in the ground to get more nutrients instead of fighting with its neighbours. By pulling two carrots out, you save the third. When you don't thin your rows at all, you end up losing all three.

Carrot seeds like to have a moist top layer of soil in order to properly germinate. This can make the process take several weeks; hot weather can slow it down even more. Water the soil before you plant the seeds and then water the area gently throughout the following weeks. As the seedlings grow, they will need to be watered as the soil dries out. This will usually be every three or four days or roughly twice a week.

Once a carrot starts to grow, it keeps growing. You can harvest tiny little carrots almost right away if you wanted, but it is best to allow them to take on their orange color. They are the tastiest when they are nice and bright. To determine the size of a carrot, carefully dig into the soil so that you can see the root. The size of the root will tell you the size of the carrot. When you are ready to harvest, use a firm grip on the root to gently pull the carrot up and out of the earth.

Growing Delicious Peppers

Peppers are one of the most enjoyable vegetables to grow because of their bright colors and iconic shape. Nothing quite says vegetable garden the same way as a fresh harvest of bell peppers does. Presenting their own challenges, peppers do best when the weather is warm and the sun spends long hours in the sky. Avoid planting peppers in shaded beds; they prefer the open sun to work on their tans.

VEGETABLE GARDENING

Peppers prefer spots that drain quickly; it is better to plant them at a higher elevation rather than at the bottom of an incline. A trellis is a smart addition to a garden bed for peppers since they like to grow tall and upwards. Attaching the plant through the trellis will allow the peppers to hang without causing too much stress on the plant. When a pepper grows too heavy, the branch it is on can occasionally break and damage the plant. It is best to plant peppers in rows. But, unlike carrots, a row of peppers should be twenty inches apart and each plant should be ten inches apart within the row itself. The soil should have a pH level between 6.2 and 7.0, which can be checked using a pH test kit or electronic pH reader. We'll discuss these in more depth in chapter four when we learn about fertilizer.

Peppers are a pretty quick crop and you can expect to start seeing them flower and fruit within a month and a half. Be mindful of the weather as they grow. Peppers can be seriously damaged when faced with a sudden cold spell. If a late spring chill is forecast, then you can cover up your plants to prevent frost damage. Keep peppers watered and supplied with enough sun and they will eventually change colors. When this happens, you are ready to start harvesting your peppers. You can then stuff them, split them, fry them or even sell them!

Growing Juicy Tomatoes

The first and most important thing to know about tomatoes is that they are going to want as much sun as possible. If you have a space that is shaded, then don't even begin considering growing tomatoes. Tomatoes need at least six hours of sunlight, but they actually want it twenty four hours, every day. They just love to soak in the sun's rays. Also, tomatoes enjoy a soil with a pH level within the 6.0 range.

Tomatoes need to have a trellis or a cage setup to prevent the tomatoes from rolling over the grow and getting bruised. A cage is easier to work with for many beginners. Some growers begin their seeds in containers and move them outdoors afterwards. Regardless of when they are planted, a tomato plant should be grown after the last frost of the spring season. Tomato plants should have a couple feet between each other; they do better in a grid arrangement rather than in rows. Tomatoes will need plenty of fertilizer but nitrogen-heavy fertilizers will slow down how quickly a plant flowers.

Tomatoes need to be watered deeply twice a week. Their root system grows quite deep underground and it needs to be watered completely. It is best to water tomatoes in the morning, so that they have moisture throughout the day. Watering after noon keeps moisture trapped in the ground overnight and creates conditions that breed sickness.

VEGETABLE GARDENING

Tomatoes are harvested late in their season. Growers want to keep tomatoes attached to the plant as long as they can before removing them. Tomatoes that fall off early might be able to be saved by being stored in a cool and dark location while they ripen. A tomato should be firm when squeezed, with a bright color. Discolored tomatoes need to be allowed to ripen and turn a deep red. If they never change colors then they never fully ripened. It is important to harvest before frost returns for the year. If you time it perfectly, you can get to have delicious, table ready tomatoes straight from the vine and plenty to store and sell.

Growing Fresh Broccoli

Broccoli is an especially great veggie to grow because it is packed full of vitamin C, beta carotene, protein, and fibre while being light on calories. As far as vegetables go, it is one of the best choices you can make to ensure you're eating healthy. It can be a little harder to grow than other green vegetables, which are leafier, like lettuce, but that doesn't mean it isn't worth the effort.

Broccoli should be planted between April and June, depending if you are looking to harvest it during the summer or during the fall. Broccoli seeds need a temperature of 50F to 85F. You can expect to see them sprouting within a week and a half from planting. Broccoli should be planted in rows that are three feet apart from each other, with plants in each row roughly three inches apart. You can grow broccoli closer together but when you do this the main heads come in much smaller; this is compensated for by an increase in the secondary heads that sprout off to the sides.

Broccoli needs to be watered heavily when it is first planted and then two to three times a week until harvest. Broccoli will need to be fertilized on a weekly basis after the seedlings are big enough, about a month after they've sprouted. Broccoli will do best with a fertilizer that has a lower ratio of nitrogen. However, you should avoid directly applying water or fertilizer onto the heads, but rather fertilize and water the soil itself. Broccoli heads rot when they are stuck in too much moisture and so it is better to be safe and avoid the possibility altogether. Note that broccoli plants have very small roots that don't poke very far under the surface of the soil and so it is quite hard to overwater them or cause them to rot. With broccoli, the risk of rot is almost entirely above the ground.

Broccoli, when starting from seed, will take between one hundred and one hundred and fifty days to grow big enough to harvest. This makes it one of the slower crops that you can plant but the nutritional value can hardly be topped. Issues like pests or disease can be unavoidable but, other than these, the biggest headache for beginners growing broccoli is rotting heads. We have already discussed how to avoid this issue. You can start growing broccoli like a pro, right out the gate.

Growing Crisp Lettuce

Lettuce is one of the easiest vegetables to grow. While we are focusing on growing it in the ground, it should be noted that lettuce does particularly well in a hydroponic system (even one as simple as Kratky's "set it and forget" system). Soil-grown lettuce will produce a smaller yield than hydroponically grown lettuce, but that doesn't mean you should avoid it. When properly cared for, lettuce can be an extremely fruitful crop both for your dinner table and your farmer's market stand.

VEGETABLE GARDENING

Lettuce is best grown in temperatures between 60F and 70F, which means it does well when grown alongside broccoli and (while not ideal) even carrots. But where broccoli takes a long time to grow and carrots like to stay on the plant for quite a while, some types of lettuce only need a month in order to fully grow. In fact, microgreens are a popular growing option which is created simply by harvesting lettuce while it is still small. You can easily have ready-to-eat lettuce in less than a month's time. This makes lettuce an incredibly fast crop, which can be great for stocking up your fridge.

Lettuce enjoys its weather to be cooler than other plants, making it one of the earlier crops you can get into the ground. Germinating the seeds will require a temperature between 40F and 85F, with the wide range speaking to the varied growing conditions of the different subspecies of the plant. Remember, you need to research your plants even after you have learned about their general care. This is because different subspecies can be on polar opposite sides of those temperature requirements. What is great for one kind of lettuce could mean death for another.

Lettuce likes to get plenty of sun; it often prefers to have full sun, but it can also benefit from some partial shade to reduce the heat if the temperature in your local area is quite high. If you are planting multiple crops throughout the year then you will need some partial shade to help seeds germinate during the summer

VEGETABLE GARDENING

months. Regardless of whether you plant it in the shade or full sun, you will want to stick with a soil that allows quick drainage and plenty of oxygen to get to the roots. Compost or manure can help improve the speed that the soil drains but these both add nutrients to the soil and you need to be careful to keep the pH level between 6.0 and 7.0.

Lettuce does just fine when started from seeds sowed directly into the soil it will be maturing in. Many plants prefer to be started in containers and allowed to grow into a healthy seedling before moving to the garden but not lettuce. This helps increase the ease of growing lettuce, as well as reduce how long it takes to bring it to harvest. Rows of lettuce should be at least a foot apart. Rather than worrying about the distance between each seed, drop ten or so seeds into each foot of the row. Remove the weaker looking plants when seedlings start to sprout so that each seedling has four inches of space around it. This is another feature that changes depending on the subspecies of lettuce, as romaine does best with twice this distance between each head. This can mean that you are removing a lot of little seedlings but these can be added to meals as microgreens and so they don't go to waste.

Lettuce doesn't need to be watered too often. You want to keep the soil moist but not completely soaked. Many plants need lots of water for their roots to grow healthy and strong but lettuce doesn't actually need deep roots. Instead of worrying about roots, the goal of growing lettuce is to produce more leaves, as they are the valuable part. A fertilizer that is balanced or even slightly nitrogen-heavy will help with this. Fertilize your lettuce once a week and water it as needed. Lettuce that needs water starts to wilt and lose its healthy fullness, so keep an eye out for these signs to lock down the best watering schedule. You want to aim to water your lettuce a day or two before these signs begin to show and so you need to listen to the plant to get a feel for how often this will be as the temperature and subspecies will impact this.

If you are a beginner who is nervous about growing their first vegetable crop, then you should start with lettuce. It is very easy to grow, is still valuable when harvested too early, and it uses its physical appearance to clearly communicate with gardeners. This can make it a learning crop to understand how plants speak to us. Plus, as an added bonus, lettuce is packed full of healthy goodness and it even has stress reduction benefits when consumed.

VEGETABLE GARDENING

Chapter Summary

- Planning a garden isn't a lot of fun but it can help you to avoid major mistakes and problems ahead of time.

- You need to consider the space you are planning to grow your garden. Each possible space is going to be a little bit different and it is important to understand what those differences are so you can match the right vegetable to the right spot.

- The elevation of a location is going to change the way that it drains. Elevated spaces will drain much quicker than spaces at the bottom of an incline, as these collect water from around them.

- Spend a day keeping track of how much sunlight the space you are considering gets. Some plants want as much sun as possible and some want very little. Knowing how much sunlight or shade a spot gets will allow you to match it better.

- Foliage or other coverage may help protect your garden from the elements and should be noted at this stage.

- Critters love eating the vegetables in your garden, and you should be aware of how they may get access to your garden and how you can prevent this.

VEGETABLE GARDENING

- Beginners often make the mistake of growing their plants too close together, which makes it hard to get to some of them. Ensure that you grow in rows or other patterns that allow you to access every plant.

- Plants in containers will need to be watered more often than those planted in the ground but otherwise their needs are remarkably similar to each other.

- It is important to take all of these pieces into consideration when deciding on where your garden should be located.

- You are free to grow anything you want in your vegetable garden, but you need to make sure that your local climate provides the right atmospheric values such as temperature, humidity, and hours of light.

- Grows plants with widely different needs in different garden beds in order for them to stay healthy.

- Carrots require a temperature of around 75F. They should be planted in rows a foot or two apart from each other, with a few inches between each seed.

- Carrots do best in a loose soil that drains quickly, though you should avoid using large minerals to increase the speed of drainage. Stick to sand or

VEGETABLE GARDENING

other smaller minerals that won't interfere with the roots.

- You need to keep the top layer of the soil moist in order for carrot seeds to properly germinate and it may take two or three weeks before you start seeing seedlings poke through the soil.

- Carrots can be harvested at any time but they taste best when they are a strong orange color. They can be left to grow to a large size but many people will harvest when they are between half an inch to three quarters an inch in diameter.

- To figure out the size of a carrot, brush the soil back so that you can see the root. The size of the root will tell you the size of the carrot.

- Peppers need warm weather. Plant them in full sun rather than shade.

- A fast draining soil is best for peppers and a trellis can make growing easier by giving support to heavy veggies as they grow. Aim for a pH level between 6.2 and 7.0.

- Rows of peppers should be two feet apart with plants ten inches apart from each other in the row.

- Peppers can grow quite quickly but you should be mindful of planting them far enough in spring to avoid a late chill but earlier enough to avoid the fall weather.

VEGETABLE GARDENING

- Harvest peppers when their color fills out and they are fully red, orange, yellow or dark green.

- Tomatoes need even more sun than peppers and so partially shaded locations will leave them unhealthy. Make sure that the soil keeps a pH level of 6.0.

- A trellis or cage should be setup to offer the fruit support. Tomatoes don't need to be planted in rows but do better in a grid pattern with a few feet between each plant.

- Tomatoes need to be watered completely as their roots grow deep under the soil. You can expect to water them twice a week but make sure it is done early in the day so that the water has enough time to evaporate before nightfall. Water that is trapped in the soil overnight promotes sickness and rot.

- Tomatoes are harvested late in the season and can be kept on the vine late into the fall season. Tomatoes that aren't fully ripe can be stored in cool, dark locations to allow them to ripen. If they never fully turn red then they haven't ripened properly and shouldn't be eaten.

- Broccoli is packed with vitamin C, beta carotene, protein and fibre. It has only a few calories per plant and so if you are growing vegetables for health reasons then broccoli is a perfect pick.

VEGETABLE GARDENING

- Broccoli needs a temperature between 50F to 85F and should be planted three feet apart with three inches between each plant in a row. Broccoli grown closer together will have smaller primarily heads but more secondary heads.

- Broccoli needs to be watered all the time when it is first planted but as it matures it moves into a twice or three times weekly watering schedule. Fertilize broccoli once a week.

- It is important now to water or fertilize broccoli heads directly as this promotes rot. Always add water or fertilizer directly to the soil instead.

- Broccoli takes between one hundred and one hundred and fifty days to fully grow, which makes it a very slow crop and not a particularly great choice for first timers.

- A better choice for first timers is lettuce, which can grow in a month or less and requires very little extra work.

- Lettuce is grown between 60F and 70F but seeds can germinate anywhere between 40F and 85F.

- Lettuce likes lots of sun but partial shade can be a good way to reduce the temperature of the plants if it is too high. Ensure that the soil drains quickly and allows lots of oxygen to the roots. Aim for a pH level between 6.0 and 7.0.

- Lettuce can be seeded in containers or directly into the ground. Plant lettuce in rows a foot apart. Drop in lots of seeds and then remove seedlings so that each plant has four inches between it and its neighbour. You can eat lettuce seedlings and so they don't go to waste.

- When lettuce isn't getting enough water it wilts and looks weaker. Try to water your lettuce a day or two before these signs appear. Lettuce doesn't need to be watered as much as some plants and they have quite shallow roots.

- Lettuce should be fertilized on a weekly basis with a nitrogen heavy fertilizer that promotes plenty of foliage growth.

In the next chapter you will learn how you go about planting those crops you have just planned. Whether it's tomatoes or carrots, you are going to need to learn about how to seed your garden. You may go straight into the ground or plant in containers, both will require a healthy soil and a careful touch.

CHAPTER THREE

HOW TO PLANT YOUR VEGETABLES

Now that you have an idea of what you want to grow in your garden, and where those garden beds are going to be placed, it is time to start seeding and planting your vegetables. Seeding and planting might seem like synonyms, but they are actually used to convey two different approaches to starting your garden.

Since our gardens are outside, in the ground, seeding refers to the act of sowing seeds directly into garden beds where they will be raised through to harvest. While this is the most common way for large-scale farming operations to start their crops, it is actually more often looked down upon by smaller scale gardeners. This is due to the fact that there is a higher risk of failure when seeding directly. While this added risk isn't overly much, it is enough to push many gardeners towards planting seedlings in beds instead.

VEGETABLE GARDENING

Planting seedlings is achieved by first germinating seeds in small containers and allowing the seedlings that sprout up to grow strong enough to be transplanted to the garden bed. While this creates an extra step and is far more time-consuming, it allows the gardener to take a more active role in the growth of their plants. Thus, the rate of successfully starting a crop is increased. However, starting seeds in containers requires more attention, time, and resources, which can make it less attractive to some gardeners.

We will be discussing both of these approaches in this chapter, as well as exploring everything you need to know about the soil that your veggies are grown in. We'll even close out the chapter with a discussion about growing your vegetables in containers and the differences that come with this choice.

Sowing Your Vegetable Seeds

Seeds are usually much easier when they start indoors but this isn't always the case. Vegetables like carrots, turnips, corn, beans, and peas are just a few examples of veggies which don't do well when started indoors. The reason that these plants don't do well indoors is that they aren't very good at handling the stress of being transplanted. This is one reason that you may want to sow your seeds directly. Another reason is the added costs that are necessary when starting seeds in

VEGETABLE GARDENING

containers indoors. If your local area is one that has short summers, then you are also better off sowing your seeds directly in order to have all your veggies in the garden and ready to soak up the sun's rays.

The first step to sowing seeds is to decide on which vegetables you are going to grow. Then you should purchase your seeds. As in soil and locations, seeds aren't all created equal. There are some species of vegetables, such as onion or corn, which have seeds that go bad after a year or so. Cabbage and carrots are among the varieties which can last up to five years, while beet and cucumber seeds can actually last much longer than five years. When you are purchasing your seeds, buy from a reputable seller who isn't going to try to unload old stock onto you. If you purchase seeds from a package, check the label to see when they were harvested. If you are purchasing them in bulk or direct from a fellow gardener then they should be able to provide you with this information. If they can't, it is in your best interest to avoid making that purchase. Low quality seeds will result in a much worse ratio of seedlings per seeds planted and any money you may have saved goes out the window when you return an underwhelming harvest.

VEGETABLE GARDENING

After you have acquired your seeds, you are likely going to need to wait a little bit. While you'll no doubt be excited about getting your seeds in the ground, it is important to make sure that the ground is ready to receive seeds in the first place. Two factors need to be in place for the soil to be deemed as ready for planting.

Depending on what time of year it is, the ground might not be warm enough for seeds yet. In order to figure out what temperature your garden beds are, you will need to purchase a soil thermometer. You can find one of these at most retail chains like Walmart, but you are better off going with a high quality one from your local gardening center or purchasing a professional one from Amazon. While you can make judgements about whether the time is right or not based on a single temperature reading, it is better to measure the temperature of the soil at different times throughout the day. Doing this gives you a much better idea of how the temperature is fluctuating. You may find that it is warm enough at noon but the mornings and evenings are still too cold. Keep in mind that the temperature you are looking for will be determined by what you want to grow; there is no one temperature that fits all vegetables. There isn't even one temperature that fits all subspecies of a vegetable. Some kinds of lettuce only need the soil to be 40F to be ready for sowing, while others require it to be closer to 85F. Always research the seeds you are going to be sowing to see what temperature they germinate at. There is a very important reason to make sure your seeds are at the right temperature. We'll come back to that after examining the second soil factor.

Making sure the temperature is right can take a fair deal of time if you purchased your seeds in winter or even early spring. The second factor shouldn't take as long, though. If you live in an area that is prone to stormy weather, then it could prove to be an issue. While many seeds want to be watered after they are planted, there aren't many seeds which you should plant into wet soil. If it has rained recently, you are going to need to wait for the soil to dry out again. There many many types of seeds which don't do well in an overly moist environment. Many prefer to have an environment in which they are provided with a little bit of water each day, but too much can cause them issues which tie into the temperature issue.

VEGETABLE GARDENING

If the temperature of the soil is too hot or too cold, then you are going to be exposing your seeds to conditions which encourage them to begin rotting. Similarly, if you overwater seeds, then you are also going to be exposing them to the same risk. Rot is a major issue that many gardeners face when they are just starting out because it seems natural to think that more water is better for the plants. You are expected to water them on a regular basis, after all. It seems logical that you could give them more water, but this doesn't check out in reality. Root rot can quickly leave your garden beds full of wilted, dead veggies if you aren't careful. When you are sowing your seeds, if you aren't mindful of the conditions of the soil, then you could be setting those seeds up to rot and never even get to see a single seedling in your garden bed.

If the soil is ready for seeds, then you have a few options available to you for how to go about this. The first thing to decide is whether you will be sowing by hand or with a tool, such as a hoe. Either choice is fine, though they have pros and cons. Sowing seeds by hand is going to ensure that every seed is properly covered and placed but it will take a much longer time. If you have a smaller garden, then this is a good choice; you're better off using tools in larger gardens. Sowing seeds by using a tool will be a much quicker experience, but you won't be able to ensure that every seed is planted properly. If you are overly enthusiastic with your hoe, then you could easily knock seeds free. The primary decision you are going to need to make when it comes to sowing seeds is whether or not you are going to be planting rows, wide rows, beds or hills. Each of these will require a slightly different approach.

Row planting is the most traditional of the approaches for a vegetable garden, though bed planting comes in at a close second. In the last chapter, we were speaking about traditional row planting when we discussed the distance between rows of vegetables. If you have already planned out your garden as suggested in the last chapter, then you will know where your rows are going. If you haven't, then consult the information in the previous chapter now.

With the placement of your rows in hand, head out into your yard with a shovel or a plough. Use these tools to make a trench down the center of the row. How deep this trench should be is determined by the type of vegetable that you are planting. Small seeds, such as pepper, carrot or lettuce seeds, are typically planted a quarter of an inch beneath the surface of the soil. Broccoli seeds are planted half an inch below the soil's surface. Some species of beans have seeds that should be planted a full inch under the surface of the soil. A general rule of thumb that you can follow is to plant a seed at a depth twice the size of its width. If you have a seed that is one eighth of an inch (like most carrot seeds are) then you will want to plant it a quarter of an inch beneath the surface. While there are exceptions to this rule, they are few and far between and this makes it one of the most useful generationalizations out there when it comes to vegetable gardening.

In a perfect world, every seed you sow would grow into a strong and healthy plant. But the world is an imperfect place and the reality of vegetable gardening is that most of the seeds you plant won't actually germinate. It is because of this that we sow a lot more seeds than we plan to actually grow. Many seeds won't take off and so we ensure that the ratio of those that do is enough to fill our gardens. This often ends up leaving us with too many seedlings growing and so we need to go through and thin them out shortly afterwards. You saw in the previous chapter that each vegetable we looked at has different space needs and so you will need to research your plants to determine how thickly populated your rows should be. You can make this thinning easier by carefully sowing your seeds with even spacing to begin with but if you are using a hoe to pack the soil back in then this is likely to push seeds around and your spacing will be slightly off.

Speaking of using a hoe to pack the soil, you may not actually need to do this depending on what you are growing. While many plants like to be covered afterwards, there are also many that don't. Tomatoes, spinach, peas, beans, broccoli, cabbage, cauliflower and peppers all like to have soil packed in above them in order to properly germinate. Among those that don't like being covered is lettuce, as it requires direct sunlight in order to germinate. However, almost every type of seed likes to be watered lightly after it has been sown. If you are planting seeds that like to be covered then you will cover them and then water them. Those that don't are just watered.

That's all there is to it. As noted, you will more than likely need to wait and thin out your seedlings as they start sprouting up out of the soil but you could argue that this is a step of maintenance rather than seeding. If you are in this camp, then you have successfully sowed seeds into traditional rows.

Sowing seeds into a wide row isn't much harder but you need to consider whether a wide row is the right option for you or not. Where a row might be a foot across, a wide row would be two feet across. You still want to dig out a trench through the middle and then sow your seeds all over the wide row. Cover the seeds if they are of the type that requires that. You'll want to try to have your seeds be about an inch or so apart from each other as you spread them out throughout the wide row.

Using a wide row isn't much harder than a traditional row though it will require you to stretch further in order to get to the plants in the middle of the row. The purpose of this is to conserve space and to make it easier to tend to the crop. Instead of having to

VEGETABLE GARDENING

go through and weed two rows and then water them after, you don't need to move around your garden as much since everything is in one space. If you don't have a lot of room for your garden then this can be a great approach but if you have the space then it is my recommendation that you plant in single rows to make it easier to ensure that each and every plant receives the proper attention and care it deserves.

If you are growing in garden beds rather than rows then you are going to follow the same steps you do to plant wide rows. It doesn't matter if these garden beds are in the ground or raised up in a frame. The main issue here is to make sure that you can reach all of your plants and so you shouldn't have a garden bed or a wide row that is any more than four feet wide. The length doesn't matter but the width is important because any wider than four feet and you will have troubles getting to your plants. While they are seeds or seedlings, this might not actually be a problem because there isn't a lot of foliage in the way. But as your plants mature, it gets much harder to maneuver through them and this leads to plants in the middle being neglected. Neglected plants increase the likelihood that you'll miss a pest infestation or the early warning signs of disease.

Finally, we come to sowing seeds on a hill. For the most part, you will want to avoid planting vegetables on a hill because your ability to control how much water they are getting is much decreased and the pull of gravity can cause issues with top heavy vegetable plants. However, plants that have lots of vines like tomatoes or cucumbers actually do quite well when planted on a hill. You'll need a trellis or a cage for these plants to support their weight but you would need these even if they were planted on flat ground. These crops do best when planted in grid formations with room between each plant. Plant a handful of seeds in a one foot area and then remove all but the strongest seedlings after they sprout. Move a foot away and do the same thing. Since each space has its own plot, you can consider each plant to be in its own unique garden bed.

Starting Seeds Indoors to Transplant Outside

Starting seeds indoors isn't necessary, but it can make the whole process much smoother and result in more healthy seedlings which you can transplant to your garden outside. However, this comes at the price of having to purchase some materials and dedicate more time and attention to the seeds throughout the germination process. This extra time and money is the only real downside of starting your seeds indoors, but there are two prime benefits which make up for the extra work.

The biggest benefit is the fact that you have a much more direct involvement in the germination and seedling stage of your plants and this will allow you to ensure that your vegetable plants are healthy before they go into your garden. When you plant directly into the outdoor soil, you are trusting your plants to the natural environment and the ebbs and flows of your local climate. This means that storms, draught, high winds, sudden frosts and exceptionally hot days are all issues that may ruin your seeds or seedlings. Since you control the growing environment indoors, you are able to remove the randomness of mother nature from the equation, which goes a long way to protect your seeds.

But the more intriguing benefit that comes from starting your seeds indoors is the fact that this allows you to start growing earlier in the season. You are going to need to wait until the last frost in early spring before you can get started growing most vegetables. This is because

VEGETABLE GARDENING

the frost kills your plants quicker than you can imagine. Frost doesn't affect your indoor plants, however. You can then start your seeds a few weeks early and have them ready to be transplanted outdoors after the last frost of the season. This means that, instead of starting from seeds at this time, you can start with seedlings that are several weeks old. This can give you a head start of a month or more, depending on how long those particular seeds take to germinate. For example, carrots may take several weeks to germinate and then a few weeks are needed for the seedlings to grow healthy enough to transplant; this means you can time it so that when other gardeners are sowing carrot seeds, you are transplanting carrot seedlings which are already six weeks old. If you are growing veggies to earn money, then this can be a major boon that can get cash coming in earlier in the year.

As mentioned, you are going to need some equipment to start your seeds indoors. You will need containers to plant the seeds in. Since these are only going to be used by seeds and seedlings, they don't need to be very big. They will need to have drainage holes in them so that water can properly seep out instead of just collecting and creating too much dampness. You will also need potting soil to fill those containers and plant your seeds in it. We'll be discussing soil later in this chapter, but there are many pre-packaged potting mixtures that will do the trick and can easily be found at your local gardening center. You will also want to get some plastic wrap to create a humid environment, as many (though not all) seeds germinate best when being provided with high humidity. Finally, you might also need to purchase some grow lights. If you have a south facing window that sees plenty of sunlight then you can probably get away without purchasing any lights. If you don't, then you will want to go with LED grow lights. Normal LED lights won't cut it because they are not formulated for use with plants. While LED lights can be a little expensive, they last longer than any other type of light and don't use very much electricity. Purchasing LED lights might be expensive at first but they pay for themselves in the long run. Equipment in hand, you are going to need to purchase seeds. As mentioned above, it is best to go through a reputable seller.

Start by filling up your seeding containers with your potting soil mixture. Some gardeners will purchase a mixture specifically designed for starting seeds; many of these don't actually contain any soil whatsoever, but rather use an inert growing media. While this approach is perfectly valid, it is better to use the same soil mixture for these seeds that you are planning to use in your garden. However, if you are adding mulch, compost or manure to your outdoor beds then you will want to leave this out. The soil will be mostly the same but it won't be quite so nutrient rich (nor will it smell as badly, which is important considering these containers will be inside for a few weeks). The reason to use the same (or similar) soil is quite simple: it will be less of a shock to your plants to be transplanted from their containers into the beds outside when the time comes. Fill the seeding containers up so that there is a half an inch between the top of the soil and the rim of the pot.

Next, plant your seeds at the depth specified either on their packaging or in the research you have done ahead of time. If the seeds need to be covered then you should do this by lightly packing the soil on top of them. It is important to note the word lightly, as soil that is too tightly packed can cut off access to oxygen, which would deprive your seeds of a necessary macronutrient. It is also worth considering why it is so important to plant a seed at the right depth. When a seed germinates and cracks open, the shell is then converted into a food source the seedling uses its nutrients in order to generate enough energy to grow roots going down and a stem growing upwards. If you plant your seeds too far down, then they aren't going to be able to get enough energy to escape from the soil. You may think that the germination was a bust, only to discover a tiny dead seedling in the soil when you go to empty out the container.

With the seed planted, it can be a good idea to cover up the container with plastic wrap. This isn't always the case, but vegetables that like a lot of humidity to germinate will benefit from this practice and it can save you from having to buy a humidifier, which is exponentially more expensive than a roll of plastic wrap. Seeds are going to need lots of water during this phase and so you will be opening up and resealing the plastic wrap a lot but once you start to see a stem and leaves forming you can remove it entirely.

Regardless of whether or not you plastic wrap your seeding containers, you are going to want to store them in a warm location. Some seeds need sunlight in order to germinate but others like to avoid light until after they are in the seedling phase. Again, you are going to need to research the vegetables you are growing to know what the right environment to provide them with is. All seedlings will need light (to varying degrees); if your seeding containers aren't already in a well-lit area, then you will need to move them to one once you notice the first leaves starting to form.

Pay attention to the temperature needs of your seedlings. As you are growing them indoors at this stage, the temperature is entirely under your control. Too warm, and your seedlings will start to fall over and not stick up properly. Too cold, and your seedlings may just freeze to death. This is just one of the many elements that you will need to note in your research prior to planting.

VEGETABLE GARDENING

If you notice that there is more than one seedling growing in a container then you are going to want to remove the weaker looking ones and keep the strongest one. One seedling per container is enough for most plants, though some smaller species can get away with two or even three. It depends on the size of the plant you are growing and not necessarily the above ground size (though this plays a part). For everything you see happening above the surface, the majority of a plant's exploration and growth happens underneath the soil as roots grow, stretch out and start to search for more nutrients. If they can't find nutrients in their immediate soil then they begin to venture either deeper or out wider. If multiple plants are left to grow in the same container then they will be fighting each other for nutrients (which take precious energy away from your healthiest seedlings) and their roots may even get tangled up together. It is best to wait until your seedlings have two separate sets of leaves before you start removing the weaker ones.

You should also start fertilizing your seedlings when you notice their second set of leaves, though it is important to note that you should only use a fertilizer at half strength or lower at this point. The reason for this is easy to understand when we consider human biology. Somebody that is 100 pounds is going to be affected stronger by a cup of coffee or a beer than someone who is 200 pounds. It is the same with plants. Larger, mature plants will be able to take a full dose of fertilizer but the smaller seedlings just can't handle it yet.

Now that you have healthy seedlings to plant in your garden, you may be getting ready to transplant them. But if you transplant them as they are then they are going to end up dead real quick. First, before you can take an indoor seedling outside, you need to harden it off. When you start seeds inside, they don't grow the necessary resistance they need for direct sunlight or protection from cold that they would have if they were started outdoors. Hardening off is the act of exposing these seedlings to the elements slowly so that they aren't shocked and quickly killed by the change.

To harden off your plants, first stop watering them or feeding them fertilizer for roughly a week prior to moving them outside. Pick a location that is protected from the wind and has either full or partial shade. This will help to introduce them to both proper sunlight and wind without overwhelming them. Take your seedling containers and set them in this spot for roughly ninety minutes each afternoon. At the end of the ninety minutes, take your seedling containers back indoors. Throughout the week prior to transplanting, give your seedlings an extra hour outdoors each and every day. By the time you are ready to transplant them, they should be outdoors for eight and a half hours at a time. You can also slowly move them from their original location in the shade to a location with more sun. A good idea is to give them full shade the first day, partial the next and slowly move them out of the partial so that they have full sun for a day or two prior to transplanting. Remember though, you don't need to give full sun to plants that are going to be growing in the shade. If they won't be in full sun when transplanted then just introduce them to the amount of sun that they will be getting in their bed. If you notice that your seedlings are wilting then you should provide them with a tiny bit of water, though not nearly as much as they receive when being watered normally. After they are transplanted they will go back to a normal watering schedule but treat the hardening off period as an aberration in their normal scheduling. If you follow these steps, then your seedlings will be ready for transplant after about a week.

It is now finally time to transplant your seedlings into your garden. This may actually be the easiest part of starting your plants indoors, but, if you aren't careful, you can cause them a lot of harm. Dig a hole in your garden for your seedling. Next, carefully remove the seedling from its container. As you do this, try not to rip or tear any of the roots. However, before you plant the seedling, you should examine the roots. Look to see if any are black and look to be slimy. Remove any that you find. This is a sign of root rot and, if you catch it now, then you can save the seedling and make it safe to plant in your garden. Place the roots of the seedling into the soil, followed by the stem and foliage. You want to pack the soil in around the seedling so that roughly the same amount of plant is sticking out above the surface as had been in the container. Some gardeners suggest adding some compost to the soil at this stage but this isn't necessary. What is necessary is to give the newly transplanted seedling a proper watering, especially because it was so parched from the hardening off process.

If you follow these steps, you should have no problems transplanting your seedlings. The most important thing to remember is the hardening step, as without it your seedlings are likely to die shortly after transplanting. There is nothing quite so depressing as heading out into the garden only to find that all your newly transplanted veggies have keeled over dead. If you properly harden your plants prior to transplanting them, you should never have to experience this.

Everything You Need to Know About Vegetable Garden Soil

When it comes to gardening, there is no piece more quintessential than the soil. While hydroponics may use an inert growing media, the image that comes to mind with gardening is that of digging through the soil. It's the part of the hobby that lets you get your hands dirty to really feel the texture of this wonderful rich soil. But, as with all things, not all soil is made equal, and you are going to want to, pardon the pun, dig a little deeper into this subject so that you know how to provide your plants with the best possible soil you can.

VEGETABLE GARDENING

Before you start sowing your seeds, you should test your soil to see how healthy it is. Most people are going to find that their backyard soil is not particularly well suited for the needs of their vegetables. They will need to substitute and augment their soil. But there are going to be rare cases where you test your soil and find out that it is absolutely perfect for your vegetables. When this happens, it is like winning the organic lottery – you can get gardening in half the time that it takes most people.

There are seventeen different nutrients which are needed for plants to grow properly. The big three are the macronutrients nitrogen, phosphorus and potassium. In addition, calcium, magnesium, sulfur, hydrogen, carbon and oxygen are also important. Plants also need the micronutrients iron, boron, chlorine, manganese, zinc, copper, molybdenum and nickel. We will use fertilizer to help feed these nutrients to our plants but the best soil has plenty of them already. Hopefully, the soil isn't too rich in these nutrients, otherwise it would cause your plants to burn out due to overfeeding (which we call nutrient burn). You want to test your soil to see if you have all the necessary nutrients and whether or not they are in the right amount or not. You can purchase a soil test kit from your local garden center or Amazon for less than $20. These tests will measure the pH level of the soil, as well as how much phosphorus, potassium and calcium is present. Some test kits will be able to tell you the nitrogen level, though not all of them have this feature. Particularly thorough test kits will be able to tell you the micronutrient ratio as well, though this often requires a more expensive purchase.

We've discussed pH level throughout the book, primarily when we looked at how to grow different types of vegetables in Chapter Two. All plants have a prefered pH level, with most vegetables falling somewhere between 5.5 and 7.5. The pH level is a measure of how acidic or alkaline the soil is. You could have soil filled with all the nutrients you need, but if the pH level was too high or too low, your plants aren't going to be able to properly absorb them. When you test your soil, you may only need to add a few nutrients back in through the use of fertilizer or compost. However, most people are going to find that their soil requires a lot of work. When this is the case, your best bet is to purchase a healthy and nutritious soil for your garden (or mix your own). This has the added benefit of allowing you to fine tune the composition of the new soil to make it drain quicker and allow more oxygen to reach the roots of your plants.

Soil texture is very important, as it determines how many gaps there are in the mixture. More gaps result in a faster draining soil that oxygen can move through easily. Soil is essentially made out of organic and inorganic elements. Organic elements are those that were once alive, like pieces of bark or compost, while inorganic elements are minerals like rock or sand. For now, you should focus on wrapping your head around the three primary components: clay, silt and sand.

Clay is the smallest component of soil and loves to stick together. Silt is bigger than clay but smaller than sand. Sand is the largest piece. You can tell these components apart by touch because soil with a lot of sand has a very rough texture, while silty soil feels like powder and soil with a lot of clay is very sticky when it is wet but coarse when dry. If you go into your backyard and start digging up the soil, you could put it to a touch test and make a fairly accurate guess as to the composition without having to get it under a microscope or study it. Soils that are heavy in sand don't have that many nutrients in them because quick draining water easily washes them out. Soils that are heavy in silt hold onto a lot of water because they have poor drainage, which results in them typically having plenty of nutrients. Soils that are heavy in clay drain poorly but don't have a lot of nutrients in them.

When it comes to growing plants, you want to balance the pros and cons of each of these elements in order to get a soil that drains quickly but also has plenty of nutrients. A good way to achieve this is to aim for a soil which equally balances these three features. If you are purchasing premixed soil then this will already be covered for you. But if you are trying to make the soil you already have work for you then you're going to want to add some organic matter to it, such as mulch, manure or compost. These will help create a better textured soil, as well as add helpful nutrients back into the soil. We will be feeding our plants a fertilizer on a weekly basis but this is a temporary fix, whereas the organic material will help keep the soil itself healthy and nutrient-rich. If you have a soil that leans too far into any one of the three types discussed rather than a more middle ground spread, you should purchase a premixed soil and use it instead.

Potting Your Vegetables

Growing your plants in pots isn't all that different from growing them in the ground when you really get down to it. Since we have covered how to start seeds in containers, there isn't a whole lot more that needs to be said. Rather than transplanting your seedlings from a container to the ground, you will transplant them from their container into a properly sized container for a mature plant of the species you are working with.

Always stick with containers that have drainage holes. While most plant pots will have these holes, this isn't true about all of them, so make sure you double check before purchasing. Also go with a terracotta or a plastic container, as these are the easiest to work with.

Growing plants in the ground will result in larger yields (if the soil is good) when compared to plants grown in containers. If your potting mixture is balanced, this isn't always true. Plants in a container are going to need to be watered much more often than those in the ground. Stick a finger an inch in the soil to check for moisture every day. Water the plants whenever you no longer feel any moisture.

Apart from these differences in care, you will pretty much be following the same maintenance steps with your potted veggies that you do with your grounded ones. However, there is a lot less digging and weeding involved in growing your vegetables in containers and you can often protect them from pests better due to the ability to move the containers around and easily separate infested plants from healthy ones. These advantages make growing plants in a container an attractive idea, even if they mean a smaller harvest.

Chapter Summary

- Seeding here refers to sowing seeds directly into the ground while planting refers to starting seeds indoors to transplant later.

- Seeds tend to take better when they are started indoors but a lot more work is involved therein.

VEGETABLE GARDENING

- Some seedlings don't take well to transplanting and so they must be started outside.

- It is important to purchase high quality seeds. Make sure either the label or the seller can tell you when the seeds were harvested.

- The ground needs to be at a certain temperature before seeds can be planted in it. It is best to wait for after the last frost of early spring.

- If the temperature of the ground is too hot or too cold, your seeds aren't going to germinate properly.

- You shouldn't sow seeds into wet soil. Wait for it to dry before sowing.

- Sowing by hand takes longer but gives you better control over the rows or beds you are seeding. Using a tool to sow will speed up the process at the cost of control.

- Planting in rows is the most common approach. Dig out a small trench, sow your seeds, cover them with soil if the species in question requires it and then water them deeply.

- Many seeds won't germinate, so it is important to plant more than you are intending to grow. You will need to thin out your rows when you do this. It is the best way to ensure enough seedlings sprout.

VEGETABLE GARDENING

- Sowing seeds in a wide bed is pretty much the same, except that you are working with a wider space. Wide beds should be no more than four feet in width.

- Garden beds follow the same rules as wide beds when it comes to sowing.

- You shouldn't sow most vegetables on a hill. It is better to set up a trellis and grow tomatoes or other viney vegetables on hills.

- Starting seeds indoors allows you to control the growing environment and provide the perfect conditions for germination, whereas starting outdoors requires Mother Nature's cooperation.

- Another benefit of starting seeds indoors is the fact that it allows you to begin your crop earlier in the year because seedlings can be started prior to the last frost of the winter.

- To start seeds indoors you are going to need soil, small containers, plastic wrap, and some LED grow lights.

- Start seeds indoors by first filling up the containers with soil. Then plant the seeds in and cover them with soil. Water them and then wrap plastic over the top.

- Seeds will need to be watered or misted. Taking the plastic wrap off for a few minutes every day also helps them to get enough oxygen. Remove the plastic wrap entirely once the seedlings start to sprout.

- Thin out your seeding containers by removing all but the strongest seedling.

- Seedlings should begin fertilization once the second set of leaves has begun to grow. Feed seedlings a fertilizer at half strength or less on a weekly basis.

- Before seedlings can be transplanted outdoors, they must first be hardened. When seeds are grown indoors, they don't form the natural protection against the elements that their outdoor siblings do. They need to be taught this.

- Stop watering your plants a week before moving them outside to harden off. Move them to an outdoor location with shade and protection from the wind. Let them stay outdoors for ninety minutes. The next day, increase this to two and a half hours while also moving the plants a little more into the sun. Continue adding an hour a day and giving the seedlings more sunlight for about a week before transplanting them. Wilting seedlings should be given only the smallest amount of water to hold them through this process.

- To transplant your seedlings, gently remove them from their container and check the roots for signs of rot. Dig a hole in the garden and

VEGETABLE GARDENING

place the seedling inside. Pack the soil around the stem to cover the roots and keep the seedling in place. Water seedlings immediately after transplanting.

- Use a soil test kit on your soil to see if it has enough macronutrients and a good pH level. Some soil test kits will even tell you how many micronutrients are present.

- Vegetables like a pH level between 5.5 and 7.5 generally. A pH level that is too high or too low will prevent your plants from being able to properly absorb nutrients.

- The texture of soil is important. You want it to be loose enough to allow quick drainage and plenty of oxygen to get the roots of your plants but also enough nutrients to keep it healthy.

- Soil is made up of clay, silt, and sand in different ratios. You want to balance these pretty evenly in your garden.

- If the soil in your yard isn't particularly fertile, then you are best off purchasing a premixed blend that has plenty of nutrients and drains quickly.

- When you grow vegetables in a pot, you start seeds in a small seedling container and then transplant them to another container instead of the ground.

VEGETABLE GARDENING

- Only use containers which have drainage holes to prevent water from stagnating at the bottom.

- Growing plants in the ground leads to larger yields, but growing them in containers can allow you more control and the ability to reposition your veggies after planting them.

- Plants grown in containers are going to need to be watered much more often than those in the ground.

In the next chapter you will learn that there is more to vegetable gardening than simply planting a few heads of lettuce. A garden doesn't grow well when it isn't properly tended. Plants require sunlight, water to drink, and nutrients to eat. If you can't provide these for your garden then it isn't going to reward you with a rich harvest. There is also maintenance to be done such as pruning away unhealthy branches or removing weeds, both of which risk the health of your garden when left unaddressed.

CHAPTER FOUR

MAINTAINING YOUR GARDEN

Your vegetable garden is now planted and in the ground. So the hard work is done, right? Not quite. From now until harvest time, you need to maintain your garden so that your veggies are healthy and happy. When they are, they will reward you with a massive yield that will leave you harvesting a ton of delicious (and healthy) treats to add to your dinner table.

In this chapter you will learn exactly what that maintenance looks like, so that you can do it with ease. We'll start by covering fertilizers, which will build on the nutrient discussion of the previous chapter to provide your plants with the necessary building blocks for a large yield. Next, we will discuss how and when to water your veggies, which happens so often that you'll be an expert by the time of your first harvest. Then we will discuss how you go about weeding your vegetable garden to remove harmful intruders that want to eat up all the nutrients in the soil. Finally, we look at a bunch of micro-maintenance which will take no time at all to do but will keep your plants healthy and happy.

How to Fertilize Your Vegetable Garden

Fertilizer is an important piece of making sure that your vegetables grow healthy and strong. However, many people seem to think that fertilizer is some kind of magic potion for plants. This results in two misinformed ideas. Some people think that fertilizer fixes all problems; instead of identifying issues such as overwatering or poor temperature, these gardeners increase the strength of their fertilizer and expect their plants to suddenly start looking healthy. The other issue is believing that more fertilizer is always a good thing. This is simply not true; in fact it is the opposite that is true. Plants being overfed fertilizer may burn themselves by absorbing too many nutrients but more often too much fertilizer messes with the pH level of the soil and makes it so the plants can't absorb any nutrients. To avoid these problems, you should always stick to the directions printed on the labels of whatever fertilizer you are using and you should educate yourself on fertilizers in general.

Alternatively, you can keep on reading to obtain all the knowledge you need to properly feed your plants.

You could mix your own fertilizer if you wanted to but this isn't recommended for beginners. It is better to purchase fertilizer that has already been formulated to meet your needs. Not only does this ensure that what you are using does what you want it to, but it will also provide you with directions on its use. Unfortunately, even purchasing a fertilizer can be a little confusing. As you're looking at bags or bottles of fertilizer you'll see a bunch of numbers that are different on each bag. This can be intimidating to some people because they instinctively think that it means they are going to have to do math but thankfully the reality is much simpler.

The purpose of these numbers is to quickly and clearly let gardeners know how much nitrogen, phosphorus and potassium are in a bag. As we saw in the last chapter, these are the three biggest macronutrients which we need to provide our plants. When discussing fertilizers, we often use terms like NPK balanced. This means that the nitrogen (N), phosphorus (P) and potassium (K) are in equal ratio to each other. Most of the time this is what we want from our fertilizer, especially if you are new to gardening. Some growers may use a nitrogen heavy fertilizer (20-10-10) or a nitrogen light one (10-15-15). This level of fine tuning requires a good knowledge of your plants' needs and the way that they will react. Experienced growers are able to make choices because they understand both how to listen to their plants and what each of the macronutrients does.

Nitrogen is used to help the plant grow. While the roots get some benefit from this, it is the leaves and foliage that gain the biggest boost. You can identify a lack of nitrogen in a plant by the way its leaves turn an autumny yellow while the rest of the plant lightens and takes on a sickly shade of green. But while a plant needs nitrogen, it will die if it gets too much. Phosphorus, on the other hand, is much more involved in growing roots and fruit. Too little of it and your plants will produce a poor yield or even fail to grow to regular size. Finally, potassium is used for more esoteric purposes such as the various chemical processes which are happening inside of the plant at any given second. Yellow leaves and a failure to grow result from too little potassium, which is

VEGETABLE GARDENING

a major pain as it can be easy to misdiagnose a potassium shortage as a shortage of either nitrogen or phosphorus.

There are two ways to apply fertilizer. Most indoor or raised bed gardeners use a liquid fertilizer. This is made by purchasing either a liquid mixture that is diluted with water or a mixture of raw materials which is then dissolved in water. This is sprayed or poured onto the soil around the plants. However, many outdoor gardeners prefer to go with a solid fertilizer which is mixed into the soil itself. One way of doing this is to mix fertilizer in with the soil as you are making rows but before anything has been planted. When done in this way, the fertilizer is mixed to be spread out throughout the soil but under the top few feet so that the plants' roots can find it as they grow. Another way is to pour a line of fertilizer along the side of the row.

The best way to determine how often and how much fertilizer to give your plants is to follow the instructions on the package. Many gardeners will start their plants off with a smaller dosage to see how they respond to it before mixing it stronger and stronger until it is at the level recommended on the package.

It should be noted that solid fertilizers don't need to be used on a weekly basis. This is the scheduling for a liquid fertilizer, which I recommend for beginners because it is harder to make mistakes with it. You could overfeed your plants, but as long as you are following the instructions it is unlikely that you will. However, a solid fertilizer can prove harmful to your plants, as direct contact with the roots while they are still young could actually just straight out kill your plants. If you use a liquid fertilizer and you are careful to follow the instructions, this won't be a problem for you. You can always branch out and start experimenting with other kinds of fertilizers after you get a feeling for how fertilizer changes the pH level of the soil and affects your vegetables. Just remember not to apply fertilizer directly to the plants but rather to the soil around them.

Watering Your Vegetable Garden

VEGETABLE GARDENING

Watering the plants is another one of the images that pop into people's minds when they think about gardening. Everyone knows that plants need water, though it seems that not everybody realizes just how much. Hydrogen is one of the macronutrients which plants need to live but too much hydrogen causes root rot and leaves your plants sick.

Too little water also leaves them sick, though it is typically better to err on the side of too little than too much. As we've discussed, your plants use visual signs in order to communicate their needs to you. One of the clear ways that plants tell us they need water is to start wilting. However, before you go watering them, you need to make sure that the reason they are wilting is the lack of water. If you notice your plants are wilting around noon, avoid watering them right away. This is the time of day when the sun is at its hottest and it may be the heat that is causing the wilt. Wait a couple hours and see if your plants bounce back as the temperature cools off. If they don't, then they probably do need watering. If they do bounce back, wilting was actually a part of the way that the plants withstand their environment. Midday wilting is the plant equivalent to people sweating a lot in the heat.

The reason you want to make sure your plants are wilting due to lack of water and not just midday heat is so that you aren't overwatering them. Your plants will give you clear signs that they are underwatered but the signs of overwatering can easily be missed if you aren't looking for them. Too much water may cause your plants to wilt as well, so remember to check the soil before watering (we'll see how this is done in a moment). Another sign is that the leaves of the plant will start to turn a brownish color and then wilt. If your plants are showing this combination of brown leaves and wilting then you can be reasonably sure that overwatering is at fault. Another sign is to look for edema, which is a condition that happens when a plant has drank too much water and its cells begin to rupture and burst. Edema shows up kinda like a blister on the leaves of the plant, though it may also look like bruises. Yellow leaves that start to fall off of the plant might be a sign of overwatering but it can be easy to misdiagnose them as a sign that there isn't enough nitrogen being absorbed.

Finally, root rot in the big one that you need to be worried about, but this starts in the roots and these are hidden from view. Root rot spreads throughout the rest of the plant, but usually by the time it enters into the foliage it is too late.

Of course, underwatering your plant can also easily kill it but most gardeners don't have a problem with underwatering. It is overwatering that does the most harm, especially to beginners who haven't done their research. It has been said a thousand times already in this book: if you want to be a gardening pro, then you need to get used to doing research. It takes next to no time and it can stop you from making deadly choices.

How often you should be watering your vegetables is going to be determined by four factors: the soil you are using, the temperature of your local climate, whether your veggies are getting full sun or shade, and the species of veggie you are growing. Oftentimes you can collapse those last two factors together because a vegetable needs a specific amount of sun or shade but there is enough variation there to make it worth the extra note. We'll discuss how these factors interact before moving on to how to tell it is time to water and how to properly water your plants when they are ready.

Out of the four factors above, the species of vegetable you are growing is going to be the most important. However, it is also the one that is the hardest to write about because of the endless variation therein. We can look to the vegetables that we discussed in chapter two to get an idea of how this changes. Carrots require weekly watering. Broccoli likes to be watered once or twice a week. Peppers like two waterings a week, same as lettuce. Tomatoes like a lot of water, twice a week. These are all pretty close to each other but you can see how carrots would be overwatered if you treated them like tomatoes. The species you are going with is your starting point; the other three factors will then alter the schedule.

Temperature and shade are tightly connected. The hotter your local climate is, the more often your plants will need to be watered. This is because heat makes water evaporate and this dries out plants quicker than cold. Whether your plants are in shade, partial shade or full sun will directly affect their temperature. You might be in a climate that isn't overly warm but your plants getting full sun will still dry out water quicker than plants which are in shade. You need to be aware that fluctuations in temperature, such as heat waves or cold patches, also change the rate of evaporation.

We come at last to soil and the role it plays in watering. We have discussed the need for quick draining soil throughout the book. How quick drainage ends up being changes drastically depending on the composition of minerals. A slower draining soil is going to need watering less often than a quick draining one, but that doesn't make it a better choice. Slow draining soil traps and keeps in a lot of moisture. This promotes the conditions for root rot and the other problems we've discussed above. So while you would need to water the plants less, you are actually making their environment more dangerous when you skimp out on the soil and ignore the need for drainage.

Now that you understand what factors change the rate that your vegetables need to be watered, you may feel like you are at a complete loss in regards to when you should water them. Twice a week makes sense but twice a week adjusted by temperature, sunlight and soil is definitely a little harder to figure out. Thankfully, there is a tried and true method that gardeners have been using for centuries to solve this exact problem. All you need to do to tell if it is time to water your vegetables is stick a finger in the soil.

This is called the finger test. Stick a finger an inch into the soil and see if you feel any moisture. You might not but this doesn't mean there isn't any. Pull your finger out and give it a look. If it is clean then the plants are dry enough to be watered. If the soil is sticking to your finger then this means that it is still moist and you should wait another day or two before watering. As simple as that is, it is the best and most accurate way to tell if it is time yet or not.

If it is time, you are best off watering your plants earlier in the day than later. This will give more time for the water to drain through the soil or evaporate back into the atmosphere. While not all of the water is going to leave this quickly, it definitely beats watering in the late afternoon or at night when the colder temperatures are more likely to keep moisture trapped in the soil threatening the health of your plants.

It is also a good idea to water your plants after a short rainfall. This might seem counterintuitive, but it makes more sense when you consider the watering instructions you are about to learn. Basically, a short shower will allow water to get a little ways into the soil but the goal with watering is to make sure that the water is going deep into the soil. A light rain shower won't penetrate very far down, so adding some water to your beds afterwards will help to turn it into a proper watering.

Depth is the goal when watering your plants. You want to make sure that the roots of your plants grow nice and deep into the ground. This requires you to get water deep into the soil. When you move a seedling into your garden, you water it immediately in this deep fashion. Essentially, what this means is that you completely soak the soil enough that the water can get far down into it. A sprinkler system or a light rain doesn't saturate the soil enough for the water to get that deep, instead it stays at the top part of the bed and quickly evaporates. This is fine for plants like lettuce which don't have deep root systems but it is doing (almost) no good for those that do.

If you follow the steps here to avoid overwatering your plants and only water them when they pass the finger test, then you won't face any of these deadly issues that seem to plague most beginning gardeners.

Weeding Your Vegetable Garden

When it comes to maintenance, you've probably noticed that fertilizing and watering your garden isn't a lot of work. You only fertilize once a week and you only water about twice a week. It would be great if growing your own delicious vegetables was this easy but the real hardship comes in weeding your garden.

Weeds are simply plants which spread naturally and don't belong in your garden. Weeds are notoriously fast growing plants and can very quickly take over a garden bed if left unchecked. They then steal energy from your plants by using the nutrients and water that would normally be used by your veggies. Large weeds or a mass of them are also able to block rays of light from breaking through to your plants. All and all, they want to leave your plants dead and take over the garden to call their own. If you are to have any chance of stopping them before they do this, you need to learn to identify them when they first arrive. Weeds are easy to tackle when they're in their earliest stages but if you don't catch them here then they can put up a long battle.

VEGETABLE GARDENING

Familiarize yourself with the weeds that are common in your local area. While you may be able to find this out on Google, your best bet is to go to your local garden center and talk to one of the knowledgeable employees there. They will be able to give you area specific information so that you know exactly what weeds you will be fighting.

Anytime you spot a weed, hack it away with a tool. Many gardeners will grab a weed and give it a sharp tug to pull its roots out. However, those roots might be intermingled with the roots of your plant and cause it damage and this negates any positive that came from removing it in the first place. Cut off the top of the weed and leave the roots alone. This may kill the intruder but some weeds are particularly resilient and can go through several such beheadings before they finally kick the bucket. This can be a long, drawn-out process but going at it this way avoids the risk of damaging your plants. Plus, depending on your mindset, it can be either really peaceful or really fun to weed a garden. Of course, some people find it neither and only consider it to be an annoyance. It just depends on the attitude you approach it with.

While it may be tempting to use a herbicide, it isn't recommended, especially if you are planning on eating or selling the vegetables from that bed. Rather, you should take the time to remove the weeds as described above. This may be a long experience but you will be rewarded for it by the rich flavors of your naturally grown veggies. While there are some natural herbicides on the market that claim to have no effect on the taste on your veggies (or no harmful effect on you), it is always better to err on the side of caution and avoid them altogether. This way you don't buy into either a lie or accidentally purchase the wrong kind and end up ruining your crop.

Other Maintenance Tasks

While fertilizing, watering and weeding are the big three, there are still a few maintenance tasks which you are going to need to do if you want to keep your garden healthy. There are also a couple tasks that you'll have to do if you want to make sure that your harvest goes smoothly and the veggies themselves are high quality. None of these tasks will take you very long, and a few of them only need to be done once, maybe twice, per crop. But skipping out on these tasks is a bad idea as doing so needlessly puts your garden at risk.

Some of these tasks could arguably be considered pest control and disease prevention techniques, such as removing dead plant matter which could harbour both. While these will be addressed in chapter six, they are important enough to merit a discussion here as well. You should be building your pest control behaviours into your general garden maintenance routine so that you are never caught unprepared by an unexpected infestation or infection.

Disinfect Your Tools After Use: This is a common sense maintenance task that you wouldn't believe how many gardeners ignore. The reason it is ignored is likely one of ignorance and a lack of knowledge. As has been stressed throughout this book, plants are living creatures. They not only have a living biology but they are able to communicate their needs to us in their own visual language. You should disinfect all of your tools, including your shovels, rakes or hoes, but you especially need to disinfect shears or anything else that has come into contact with the plants themselves. Trimming a plant is essentially a form of surgery. Imagine going in for an operation and finding out the surgeon used a dirty scalpel to cut you open. You wouldn't be surprised at all when the wound got infected or you caught a new disease. Yet many gardeners leave their tools dirty and use them again and again, only to be surprised when their plants end up sick. Always disinfect your tools at the end of the day after using them.

Remove Dead Plant Matter: Another step that is often forgotten about is the removal of dead plant matter. A lot of beginner gardeners don't see a problem with a dead plant matter in their beds. This is pretty easy to understand; after all, it is just matter that has fallen off of your plants and so why would they think it was harmful? But leaving dead plant matter in and around your garden is one of the worst things you can do if you want your plants to stay healthy. The problem isn't the dead matter itself. The plant matter is dead, it's not going to do any harm. The problem is in what this matter attracts. Dead plant matter is a breeding ground for pests and disease. Pests can hide in this plant waste, feeding off it while it is still fresh and then moving on to your plants shortly afterwards. It is a good idea to check your garden daily to clear out your dead. If this is too much work for you then at least clean out the beds whenever you go to water them. As long as you don't let any dead and rotting plant matter stick around for too long, you will probably be okay. It is not a guarantee that you will be, of course, though neither is removing it daily. It just drastically lowers the chances.

VEGETABLE GARDENING

Set Up Shade: Despite the fact that you may be growing plants that love direct sunlight, there may be moments when the heat is too much for them. When faced with a heat wave, these plants may get burned or damaged. You should be checking the weather not only every day but also the extended forecast. If there are spikes in the temperature, you may need to set up shade for your plants. This isn't actually done to reduce the amount of sun the plants are getting (though this is a result of it), but rather to bring the temperature of the plants down a few degrees. Full sun veggies are going to want that sun, but they can handle a couple days of shade better than they can handle being burnt to death.

Offer Support: While plants like tomatoes, cucumbers or peppers are going to require a trellis, there are many other types of vegetables that can benefit from using one as well. It can be particularly useful to use trellis on plants that have a lot of foliage. These plants tend to spill out and stretch their leaves far and wide. A trellis can be used to contain this spread and keep your garden looking much neater. This has the added benefit of making it easier to get in and work on the plant when it is time to trim, harvest or check for pests. The plant actually gets several benefits. Because the trellis keeps it upright, more of the plant will be exposed to the sunlight, which can help with growth. This also allows the plant in question to more easily get oxygen to the roots because the foliage is lifted off of the soil and so it no longer blocks possible entry routes in and through the soil.

Add Mulch to Your Garden: Mulching your garden means adding a layer of material to the top of your garden. Popular materials for mulch are grass clippings, straws, shredded bark, sawdust, woodchips, shredded newspaper, cardboard and so much more. When it comes to vegetable gardening, the best mulch you can use is straw. This layer helps slow the drainage of the top part of the garden bed and makes it harder for weeds to take hold as seeds are much more likely to get trapped in the mulch layer rather than get into the soil proper. This also helps keep your plant's roots cooler, which can help during heat waves. Mulching can be done for aesthetic reasons too, as a colored mulch can really make your landscaping pop. Add mulch to your garden after your seedlings have grown at least two sets of leaves. Keep an eye on your mulch and replace it as it begins to decompose. It isn't as big of a deal with vegetables since they are dug up so often but you shouldn't leave mulch on a bed for more than half a decade.

VEGETABLE GARDENING

Chapter Summary

- Fertilizer is an important part of keeping your vegetables growing big and healthy, but it isn't a miracle substance. If you have problems with pests, temperature, overwatering, or anything else of the sort then fertilizer isn't going to help in any way.

- Too little fertilizer may result in smaller plants, but too much fertilizer is a recipe for dead plants.

- Many experienced gardeners mix their own fertilizer but it is better for beginner's to purchase their fertilizer premixed so that it has the right ratio of macronutrients.

- Fertilizer is primarily concerned with nitrogen, phosphorus and potassium (NPK). Most fertilizers will list three numbers like 10-10-10, which tells you the amount of nitrogen, phosphorus and potassium in that order.

- Many premixed fertilizers will also have micronutrients, but these are more often found in the smaller print on the back of the label.

- Nitrogen primarily helps plants to grow lots of leaves and foliage.

- Phosphorus is used to help the roots and the fruits grow

VEGETABLE GARDENING

- Potassium is concerned with chemical processes inside the plant and is used to generally keep it healthy.

- Fertilizer can be bought as a solid spread which you mix directly into the soil of the garden bed or as a liquid. It can also be a mix that can be dissolved in water.

- Liquid fertilizer offers beginner gardeners more control over application and this leads to less accidents and overfeeding.

- Always follow the instructions on the label when deciding how much fertilizer to use.

- Solid fertilizers don't need to be applied on a weekly basis.

- Underwatering your plants will leave them wilting but it is actually much better to underwater than it is to overwater.

- Many plants wilt a little around midday when it is hottest. This isn't a sign of underwatering but rather a natural process that helps them survive. Always check that a plant is still wilting a few hours later before rushing to water it.

- Overwatering your plants can lead to brown and wilting leaves; edema, or little blisters and bruises on the leaves; leaves that turn yellow and then fall off; or root rot, which starts under the soil

VEGETABLE GARDENING

but moves up through the foliage to quickly kill the plant.

- Underwatering can lead to the death of the plant but nowhere near as quickly as overwatering does.

- Your watering schedule is determined first by how often the species in question is supposed to be watered. This rate is then increased or decreased depending on the soil it is growing in, the temperature of the local climate and how much sun it is getting.

- How quickly the soil drains is important because slow-draining soil traps moisture in longer and can be dangerous for your plant's health. The higher the temperature, the more often you will need to water. The lower the temperature, the less often. Plants in full sun beds will require more watering than those in the shade because the direct sunlight facilitates evaporation.

- To tell if a plant is ready to be watered, stick your finger in the top inch of the soil. If it is moist to the touch then it isn't ready. If you pull your finger out and soil sticks to it, it isn't ready to be watered yet.

- It is better to water plants earlier in the day rather than later, so that the water has time to move away from the roots or evaporate before the cooler temperatures of night that can trap the moisture in the soil.

VEGETABLE GARDENING

- Watering your plants after a small rainfall is a good idea so that they are deeply watered, which promotes root growth.

- Water your plants so that the soil is saturated. Some gardeners purchase sprinkler systems for their vegetables but this isn't actually very helpful. A sprinkler is great if you're trying to keep your grass green but vegetables are going to need to be deeply watered.

- Weeding your garden is the longest step of maintenance but it is equally as important as fertilizing or watering.

- Weeds are fast growing plants which steal the sunlight, water and nutrients from the other plants in your garden.

- Many people yank weeds out of their gardens to get the roots out but this can cause damage to the roots of the plants you are trying to grow. It is better to cut the heads off of roots and let the roots die. Some weeds have to be "beheaded" several times before they finally give up.

- The best way to learn about what weeds are in your local area is to head to your local gardening center and ask one of the employees.

- It is important to be able to identify weeds on sight, especially when they are young and only starting to sprout. Spotting them early can allow

VEGETABLE GARDENING

you to kill them off before they can stage a full-blown invasion of your vegetable garden and greatly cripple your crops.

- You can use herbicide to kill weeds but this can have a negative effect on your vegetables and so is best avoided.

- You should always disinfect your garden tools after you use them in order to remove any harmful bacteria or viruses that might be on them. Otherwise, you might introduce sickness to your garden the next time you use those shears or that shovel.

- Dead plant matter that has fallen off of your veggies is not harmful in and of itself but it creates a space for pests and disease to fester and grow. It is a good idea to remove dead plant matter every day. If this is too much work then remove it at least every time you water your garden.

- Even plants that like full sun can be damaged during a heat wave. Keep an eye on the weather channel to get a heads up about temperatures throughout the week and set up shade to help your full sun plants through extra hot days.

- While plants like tomatoes need a trellis, many plants that can grow just fine without one and actually do really well when a trellis is used. The benefits of using a trellis include clearing up space, allowing more oxygen to the roots and

VEGETABLE GARDENING

exposing more of the plant to soak up the rays of the sun.

- Mulch is added to the top of a garden to help reduce weeds, trap water and keep roots cooler. It can also be added for its aesthetic value.

In the next chapter you will learn how to harvest the vegetables that you are growing in your garden. Harvested veggies can go straight to the dinner table but often there will be just way too many of them to eat all at once. When this is the case, you need to know how to preserve those veggies so you can have them throughout the year.

CHAPTER FIVE

HARVESTING AND PRESERVING

We've finally gotten to the most exciting time for any new gardener. At long last, you have made it to the harvest. You were able to sow your seeds, bring them through to maturity and keep them alive through careful maintenance. You're now looking at a garden full of beautiful and tasty looking vegetables that you can't wait to dig into.

Only, there's one small problem. You don't know just how you are supposed to start harvesting the fruits of your labor. What's more, you miscalculated and actually have a much larger yield than you were expecting. There's no way you can eat all those veggies before they go bad. The good news is that you can preserve many vegetables for a decent length of time. You might not be able to eat them all but you can eat a bunch, sell a bunch and gift a bunch to your friends and family.

In this chapter we will explore how to do exactly that. From telling it is time to harvest to the actual harvesting itself, through to preversing your vegetables for later consumption, everything you need to know to get those veggies on your dinner plate tonight is covered below.

How to Tell it's Time to Harvest Your Veggies and What to Do When It Is

When it comes to harvesting your vegetables, you've probably already figured out that each kind you grow is going to have different harvesting needs. In order to accommodate this, we will be looking at a bunch of different veggies to see what unique signs they give us to let us know they're ready for harvest. But before we do that, there are a few tips to help us with the harvest. After we know that it is time to harvest our veggies, we'll take a look at how to harvest the more popular ones.

The first thing you need to know about harvesting is that a bigger vegetable isn't necessarily a better vegetable. Of course, we all love it when we can get nice big veggies because there is more eating to be had but vegetables like lettuce and spinach, cucumbers and beans, peas and potatoes are all tastier when they are harvested a little earlier when they still haven't fully matured. Now there are vegetables (like tomatoes)

VEGETABLE GARDENING

which are best when they are properly given time to mature but "bigger is better" only applies to certain veggies and not the whole garden.

You should also not harvest when the soil is wet or when it is raining. It is always better to give your plants some time to dry off before you start picking vegetables off them. This weather leaves the plants more vulnerable to disease and so they need their full strength to stay healthy. If you start picking at them, you will stress them out. This stress isn't very harmful while the environmental conditions are right but when they are wrong and there is a lot of moisture around, you are inviting danger into your crop. You might think this doesn't matter because you are harvesting and so you won't need that crop any more but this is wrong.

VEGETABLE GARDENING

You don't just harvest your vegetables once and move on. In fact you should harvest them over the course of several days or even several weeks. Not every vegetable on a plant matures at the same time. The oldest veggies will mature first and need to be harvested earlier. Removing these from the plant will then help it to send energy towards the remaining veggies to speed up how fast they mature. By harvesting several times, you will end up with a bigger and better yield because of the way you are taking control of how the plant spends its energy.

With these tips in mind, let's turn our attention over to specific vegetables and check to see if they are ready to harvest yet.

Asparagus: Asparagus grows in shoots that are referred to as spears. They are ready to harvest when they are roughly the size of your hand and as thick as your little finger. Grab each spear tightly by the base as close to the soil as you can get. A quick twist will snap them off. The best part of harvesting asparagus is that new spears will continue to grow from the part left in the ground. Harvesting asparagus should last a month, maybe a month and a half. While you may still see new spears popping up, we stop harvesting so that the plant is able to heal up for later use.

Beans: The most common bean you'll find in a North American vegetable garden are snap beans. It can be hard to judge the right time to pick these because you don't look for a sign to tell it's ready; rather, harvesting snap beans is about picking them before signs start to show up. As these beans mature, the seeds inside of them start to bulge out more and more. The more they bulge out, the tougher the bean is and the less tasty people generally find it. You can pluck these right off the plant itself and you are going to want to try to harvest them before you notice the seeds starting to really bulge out. If you have harvested them at the right time then you should be able to snap the bean it half with your bare hands, which is also how they got their name.

Beets: Everytime we seed the garden, we are going to sow more seeds than we need. Most of these plants will be thinned out. Beets are a cool veggie because you can actually eat the green tops that you remove at this step. For the beets that stay in the ground, keep an eye on the soil and wait until you see their shoulders start to poke out. When this happens, you can harvest the beets. However, you don't need to harvest them immediately. Beets can be left in the ground to grow quite large, so you will need to use your own taste test to decide which size is the best for your dinner table.

Broccoli: Broccoli is a bit of a weird one. You don't want the flowers to bloom and so what we do with broccoli is remove the flowers while they are still buds. But, just like the green part of beet seedlings, this is actually a part that we can eat. They taste particularly good when fried up with a little bit of butter. You don't really find broccoli buds at the supermarket, so this is a snack almost exclusively experienced by gardeners. As for the broccoli itself, you shouldn't expect yours to be the same size as the stuff you buy at the store. Take six inches of the stem and cut it when the buds at the end are the size of the eraser at the end of a pencil. While the main bit will not grow back in time to be harvested a second time, smaller secondary heads will continue to sprout and this will give you more broccoli to harvest and snack on while you take care of the rest of your veggies.

Brussel Sprouts: When it comes to brussel sprouts, you can expect to be harvesting them over a long period of time. As mentioned above, the older sprouts will mature and be ready for harvest sooner and so you will start harvesting from the bottom to make your way up to the top. Make sure to check them every day because they can quickly go from immature to mature in the course of a night during the harvest season. Sprouts should be an inch thick before you begin to harvest them but when they are all you need to do it grap the stem and twist it off the branch. If you don't have good grip strength then you can easily use a small pair of shears to clip them off the stem.

Cabbage: Remember how we said that bigger isn't always better? Cabbage is a great example of this. They are easy to harvest, just pull the head out of the ground and you are good to go. It is even easy to tell when it is time to harvest your cabbage. Just grab the cabbage head and squeeze it a little. If it is soft and malleable then it needs time to mature. If it feels solid and firm (but not rock hard) then you can just pluck it out the ground right then. But if you want to leave your cabbage in the ground to grow even bigger, you're going to have a bad time. You'll come back to find that your crop is ruined. The goal of leaving it in the ground would be to harvest a bigger head of cabbage. But what will happen is the cabbage will continue to grow and split apart and lose a lot of the flavor. When it is harvest time, be very careful to check each head and pluck them as soon as they feel ready.

Carrots: As we discussed in chapter two, carrots are one of those vegetables that can be left in the ground well after they have fully matured. The bigger is better concept definitely can apply to carrots. But that said, it depends on what you are after. If you want to grow baby carrots, then you are going to be harvesting your carrots far earlier than someone who is after big ones for dicing and slicing. To check the size of a carrot, you need to brush back the soil to take a good look at how thick it is. While a carrot that is a good thickness will most often be a good length, this isn't always the case and you won't know for sure if they are long enough without checking. Start with a single carrot. If it is too short then eat this one and leave the rest in the ground for a few more days before checking another. Repeat until your test carrot is the size you are looking to harvest.

Cauliflower: Cauliflower grows nice and thick when it is ready to be harvested but it is another one that can be left too long and start to degrade in quality. The cloud-like ends of each head should still be smooth when you harvest. If the heads start to become rough and uneven then it won't taste quite as good but you can still harvest and enjoy some. This makes cauliflower one of those veggies like snap beans, that you need to harvest before you see a sign rather than after.

Corn: After the green silk forms at the end of your corn stalks, you can expect them to start turning a brown color and drying out. While this would be a sign of disease in another plant, this is a sign that you should be checking the ears to pay close attention for the moment of harvest. Use something sharp to cut into a kernel. If nothing comes out then it isn't ready yet. But if a pale liquid oozes out then you are ready to start harvesting. Grab the ears, give them a sharp twist and then pull them off.

Cucumber: Bigger is not better with cucumbers and it is much better to harvest them a little younger compared to overly mature. If they are left too long then cucumbers start to taste bitter and lose their texture. Keep an eye on your plants when it is around harvest time. The cucumbers will start small and kinda twisted, so when they are nice and smooth you can tell they have come into their proper size. Give them a squeeze; if they are still soft then they will need another day. Maybe two, but rarely three. Cucumbers have a tight window of harvesting that's pretty much the complete opposite of carrots. This can make them a hard crop for beginners to properly harvest without lots of care or knowledgable help.

Eggplant: While you can just grab corn and twist it off, eggplants should be carefully removed from the plant with a careful cut. You will also want to harvest them early rather than late. They don't go bad quite as fast as cucumbers do but they behave in a similar fashion. Eggplants are harvested in a window of time after they have hardened up inside but still have their deep purple shine to them. If they are starting to lose their shine, you should start the harvest immediately or their flavor will greatly diminish.

Garlic: The sign that garlic is ready to harvest may be confused for signs of disease because the top part will grow a brown color and begin to wilt. While this is a terrible sign in most vegetables, it is the opposite in garlic. If you see this prior to the harvesting window then you have a problem, but if you see it during the harvest season you have the fixings for a steak. When you spot the wilted brown tops, dig up the bulbs and brush the dirt off. They'll need to be left to dry but you can be adding them to your diet within a day.

Head Lettuce: Head lettuce is much like cabbage, just squeeze the top to see if it is firm or soft. Soft isn't ready, firm might be but if it feels like it isn't very full then you probably have a couple days left to go. It is better to harvest earlier than later if hot weather is on the horizon. You should be making it a habit to check the weather every day anyway, but if you are growing lettuce then this is a must because hot spells can actually cause lettuce to stop filling out and instead go to seed. Lettuce can be harvested pretty much anytime to enjoy some microgreens so harvest before hot weather regardless of size.

Kale: Kale is a very popular veggie these days because it is super healthy and tastes great in a smoothie.

VEGETABLE GARDENING

The cool part with kale is that you can pretty much pick from it the whole time. While you could just harvest the plant in full, if you take from it slowly then it will live longer and you can get much more from it. Like lettuce, you should harvest kale before warm weather comes. For kale this is to keep it tasting the best. Don't begin cutting and taking from it until the leaves are firm and take on a dark shade of green.

Leaf Lettuce: Wait until leaf lettuce grows to the size of your middle finger and then start harvesting from the outside in. By going this way, you give each successive layer of leaves more time to grow. Like kale, you can harvest leaf lettuce during the entire harvest season. Unlike kale, leaf lettuce doesn't mind the hot weather the same way its heady cousins do.

Leeks: Leaks are a really cool veggie because they can survive in the ground throughout the winter. If you are looking to use your garden as your primary source of vegetables then leaks give you one that you can harvest in the winter. When leaks are about an inch thick, simply dig them out of the ground.

Onion: Onions are like garlic in that wilting during harvest season is a sign that they are ready, not that they are having problems. Once you see the top part of the onion has fallen over, simply dig them up and let them dry out for a bit in the sun.

VEGETABLE GARDENING

Parsnip: Parsnips are similar to leeks in their ability to survive throughout the winter. However, they are best left to harvest in the warmer spring weather rather than during the winter. If you are looking for another crop to get you through the winter, parsnips are a good choice because they actually taste way better when they're harvested after a few frosts. For winter purposes, harvest parsnips as close to the first snow as you can. They're like carrots in that they'll continue to grow in size while in the ground so this gives you the biggest and the tastiest parsnips you possibly can get without waiting until spring. Dig them out like you would carrots.

Peas: Harvesting peas is a lot like harvesting snap beans but with peas you want the peas inside to develop and fill out. The longer peas after left on the plant, the less sweet they become. Once you start feeling peas in the pods, begin taste testing them and harvest them when you think they are the right sweetness.

VEGETABLE GARDENING

Potatoes: While potatoes grow underground, you don't have to dig them up to check them like you do carrots. Instead, wait until the green foliage on top of the soil starts to flower. They can be harvested any time after this but they will be largest when the tops have lost their color. It can be very easy to damage your potatoes when harvesting them. Unlike carrots, potatoes are directly attached to their foliage and they may have spread out throughout the soil in any direction.

Radishes: Like beets, you look for the shoulders of the radish to start breaking out of the soil before you harvest. However, radishes actually grow a lot faster than beets and so you will be harvesting them sooner and more often, too. Unfortunately, despite being grown in the ground, they also quickly get tough and tasteless if they aren't harvested soon enough. Radishes are best planted a few each day over the course of a week or two so that they aren't all harvested at once.

Spinach: When the spinach plant is as tall as your middle finger, you can start plucking off the smaller leaves. These taste great and they allow larger leaves a chance to get more energy redirected to them before the proper harvest. Unfortunately, spinach can be a bit hard to time because you want to harvest before new stalks sprout up and start growing flowers. Use shears to cut spinach at the stem to remove all the leaves at once.

Squash: You can grow either summer squash or winter squash. Summer squash needs to be harvested when it has filled out but is still soft enough that you can poke a sharp object through the skin without any issue. Winter squash is ready to be carefully cut off of the plant once its color has filled out completely. Despite the name, winter squash simply cannot survive frost and needs to be harvested beforehand.

Tomatoes: We talked about tomatoes in more depth in chapter two but they are harvested when they have completely turned red. They should be squishy when squeezed; if firm, much of the flavor will be absent. Tomatoes also smell like tomatoes, making them one of the vegetables that most activate this sense during the harvest. Take tomatoes in hand and twist them off from the plant, being careful not to squeeze too tight and burst them.

Turnip: Turnips are like beets and radish, the shoulders are ready to harvest when they are as wide as your pinky is long. It is better to harvest a turnip a little bit early than a little bit late as they take on an unappealing taste if they are in the ground too long. Dig away at the soil and pull them out of the ground to harvest.

How to Preserve Your Freshly Harvested Vegetables

There are four main methods that are used for preserving vegetables. These include drying, canning, pickling and freezing them. While we could look at them in any order we wanted, this particular order reflects their order of invention as each method required new technologies to be invented. As with many things, we have more options for preserving our food these days than we ever did before. Funny enough, sometimes the old fashioned ways are the most appealing, such as is seen in the rise of canning as a hobby in the past few years.

VEGETABLE GARDENING

Drying: The moisture in plants contributes greatly to their rotting and going bad. Drying out all of the moisture is one way to preserve a harvest. Of course, this greatly changes the flavor of the vegetable. While not a vegetable, the perfect example is raisins. Delicious, but they taste nothing like the grapes they were before being dried out. As moisture leaves, the texture changes entirely. While drying is mostly done with fruit, it can be used with vegetables too. It is the most primitive way of preserving food but not necessarily the worst. It just depends on whether you enjoy the new texture and taste of the vegetable or not.

The first step to drying is to clean the vegetables. You don't want them to be dirty during this process because it can easily get trapped and you'll find yourself biting into it later on. People have ever chipped their teeth this way, so always wash your yield. But they also shouldn't be wet, so pat them dry.

Next, you are going to want to blanch your vegetables. This is done by cooking your vegetables in boiling water for a very short time. Small vegetables only need a minute, but larger ones will need longer and really thick ones may take up to ten minutes. You will need to research this for the particular vegetable you are looking to blanch but there are many resources for this for safety reasons. Cook a pound of vegetables in four litres of water. Wait for the water to boil, then put in the vegetables. Start watching the time once the water begins to boil again and remove them based on the food safety guides. You will also need to blanch foods to freeze them, but not for pickling or canning.

Next comes the actual drying. This used to be done using a flame oven and camp fires but nowadays we can use our ovens. You don't want to turn it on very high, pretty much keep it at the lowest. Spread out some cooking tissue over a baking tray and then lay out the vegetables you are going to be drying. You will want to be very careful to keep pets and children out of the kitchen while you do this because when you stick them in the oven, you leave the door open a bit. This can turn dangerous really fast if you aren't careful. Tomatoes and peppers can take up to a day to dry, though some plants take only a couple of hours. It is best to group drying vegetables together by size or keep everything to one type at a time.

After you have dried out your vegetables, you need to seal them into an airtight package in order to prevent any moisture from getting back into them. This is most often done with bags or jars. For the best results, you want to match containers to the size of the vegetables. The less free space, the better. Things will jostle around less and the vegetables will keep their favours much longer.

While you'll likely be unable to watch the oven for a full 24 hours without taking a break, you should check on drying vegetables often to make sure they are drying and not just baking. Leafy greens and other vegetables on the lighter end (as well as herbs) should start to crumble but not fry. Bigger vegetables like tomatoes start to dry out until you can snap them in half. Researching how to dry a particular vegetable will tell you how long it needs and even show you photos of how it should look when it is done. If done properly you can save vegetables for a close to a year.

Canning: Canning is best used for pickles, salsas, tomatoes or other pastes and jams. This makes it a less useful technique for many of the items that make up a vegetable garden. It is also the hardest of the techniques used to preserve your yield. However, it does prevent mould or other harmful pathogens from getting in.

This method isn't recommended for beginners but if you are going to consider it then remember that what you are canning needs to be ripe and your jars need to be in good shape. Any nicks or scratches that air can get into will ruin your canned veggies.

Pickling: While cucumbers are the first vegetable to jump to mind, many other veggies can be pickled, like carrots or cabbage. This will greatly change their taste but it can add some great flavors to a meal and will keep for months. Fermented pickles take weeks in order to be ready to eat and go beyond the realm of the beginner. But if you want delicious pickled vegetables that keep in the fridge then there is a much simpler method which you can follow. These pickles will last a couple months but they are easy to make.

Use glass jars for pickling. The first thing you are going to do is bring them to a boil. Make sure that you also boil the lids with the jars. This will kill off any bacteria and germs that are on them so that nothing goes wrong with the process. Simply put the jars into one pan and the lids into another and bring them to a boil. Give them a minute, then turn off the stove and wait until they cool down.

VEGETABLE GARDENING

While the pan is cooling down, you should begin preparing your vegetables. Peel off the skins and cut them up so they will fit into the jar. You can do these as strips or chunks or anything in between but keeping them roughly the same size will have the best results. When you have enough vegetables to fill up a jar, safely remove one from the pan. Drop your vegetables inside and continue chopping up for the next one. Fill up all of the jars before moving on.

When you finish cutting, measure out a cup of vinegar and put it in a pot on medium heat. Mix in a tablespoon of salt and mix it until you can't see it anymore. Measure a cup of water, mix it in and quickly take the mixture off the stove. The vinegar will have gotten a little warm but the water will cool the whole thing down. Pour this into the jars with the veggies until the jar is completely full. Put the lid on nice and tight as soon as it is no longer hot (from the boil). Stick the jars in the fridge and give them a couple hours to cool down further before trying them.

You can add spices or herbs to your pickled vegetables if you want to give them a distinct flavor. Simply add spices or herbs to the jars before you mix in the pickling juice. There are tons of different flavors that can be achieved through pickling. While it changes the natural flavor of the vegetable, pickling does offer plenty of amazing experiences for the palate to discover.

Freezing: The newest method available to us, freezing, is also super easy. The ability to freeze food wasn't available to many of our ancestors but they certainly would have wished that it was. The simple act of freezing your food can allow you to keep your vegetables for a year or more depending on the veggie in question.

VEGETABLE GARDENING

You are going to need to cut your veggies and remove shells, stems, and anything that isn't going to be eaten. Once you have done this, prepare and blanch the veggies, which we covered above as part of drying. Vegetables need to be given time to cool back down after being blanched. You may want to speed this process along, if this is the case then you can use ice water to cool down the veggies. Don't move to the next step until they're cool.

You are going to need some freezer bags to stuff your vegetables into. Stove in the veggies and then close them carefully, letting out as much air as possible in the process. This can be done by hand but people who are freezing a lot of vegetables may want to get some mechanical aid from a vacuum sealer.

VEGETABLE GARDENING

VEGETABLE GARDENING

Chapter Summary

- Harvesting your vegetable garden is the most time-consuming part of the whole process because you need to be checking it daily and looking out for certain signs and reacting quickly.

- By learning how to preserve your vegetables you will be able to keep your table packed high with nutritious food all year long.

- Different types of vegetables are harvested at different times throughout the year and have different signs that signal when they are ready. You will need to research your specific veggies to know what is best.

- Vegetables aren't always better when they are bigger. There are some kinds that are tastier when they are harvested a little early and there are some that go bad and lose their flavor if they grow too big.

- Never harvest in wet soil. If it rains, give the soil enough time to dry out so that you don't risk exposing your plants to disease.

- Many vegetables can be harvested throughout the season rather than just at one time and so you can get a lot of eating out of your veggies by carefully harvesting. Always remove the oldest

VEGETABLE GARDENING

parts of the plant first to allow younger parts to grow.

- Asparagus is ready to harvest when it is the size of your hand. Break it off by the soil and continue harvesting it as it grows back.

- Beans need to be harvested before they start to bulge out.

- You need to remove broccoli flowers throughout the season but these can be cooked and eaten. Harvest the broccoli itself when the buds are the size of an eraser. Secondary heads will continue to grow and can be eaten as well.

- Brussel sprouts mature very quickly and they are harvested all throughout the season.

- Cabbage needs to be firm and full but not too full. If left in the ground too long, then they will start to crack and split.

- Carrots can be harvested pretty much any time. Check the size of the root to get a feeling for the size of the carrot. Just because a carrot is the right thickness doesn't mean that it will be long enough. Carrots can stay in the ground for as long as you want before winter and so if they aren't big enough, then just give them a few more days.

- Cauliflower is harvested when the heads are full but smooth.

VEGETABLE GARDENING

- When the silk corn husk starts to turn brown then you can begin checking the kernels. When a cut kernel starts to leak a milky substance, it is time to start harvesting.

- Cucumbers are harvested while they are still young in order to have the best flavor.

- Eggplant should be cut off the plant when it is smooth with a deep purple shine.

- The top of garlic turns brown and collapses when it is time to harvest the cloves.

- Like cabbage, head lettuce should be full and firm but it is better to harvest it a little early rather than keep it in the ground during warm weather.

- Kale can be picked throughout the harvest season. When picked only a little at a time, it lasts a remarkably long time and provides tons of nutritional value.

- Leaf lettuce can also be picked throughout the harvest season, starting from the outside in for the best results.

- Leeks can survive in the ground through winter. Similarly to carrots, simply dig them out of the ground when they are an inch thick.

VEGETABLE GARDENING

- The top of the onion plant wilts when it is ready to be harvested. Carefully dig out the onions and let them dry in the sun before taking them inside.

- Parsnips can stay in the ground throughout the winter and actually taste better after a few frosts.

- Peas need to develop in the pod before they are picked but they should be taste-tested often so you can harvest when they are the sweetest.

- Potato plants start to flower when they are ready for harvest but you need to be extra careful digging them out of the soil because they are easy to damage.

- Radishes are harvested based on the size of their shoulders. It's better early than late with radishes because they lose their flavor when left in the ground too long.

- Spinach can be picked a bit at a time while growing so that it provides plenty of eating even before you harvest it fully.

- Squash needs to fill out and take on its color before it is harvested by being cut from the plant.

- Tomatoes should be entirely red before you twist them free from the vine.

VEGETABLE GARDENING

- Turnips are ready to harvest based on the size of their shoulders and also take on a gross flavor if left too long.

- Drying out your vegetables requires you to clean them, blanche them, and then leave them in the oven on low for a few hours up to a whole day. This will bake out all of the moisture in them so that they can be kept for up to a year but it will change their flavor drastically.

- To blanch your vegetables is to cook them in boiling water for a short period of time. This is important for drying and freezing and there are lots of health guides that can be found on the topic thanks to its importance to storing food.

- Canning is a complicated method used to create an airtight environment that can be used to store tomatoes, salsa, pickles, and pastes or jams. Canning isn't recommended for beginners.

- Pickling can be done to a lot of different vegetables, though it will change their taste. Boil glass jars and their lids to kill off any germs and then fill them with cut up veggies. Dissolve a tablespoon of salt into some vinegar and then add a cup of water. Fill up your jars with the liquid mixture, adding any spices you want to include beforehand. Stored in the fridge, these pickled vegetables will last several months.

VEGETABLE GARDENING

- Freezing your vegetables is the best way to preserve them without drastically changing their taste. Blanch your vegetables before storing them in freezer bags. Squeeze out as much of the air as you can before sealing so that these frozen vegetables can last up to a year.

In the next chapter you will learn how to take preventative steps to avoid having to deal with pests and diseases that are common problems when growing vegetables. These steps will all be organic and green, so there won't be chemical insecticides poisoning your crops. You'll also learn how to deal with common pests in case the preventative measures fail. Dealing with pests and disease is a common experience and so it is important for beginners to learn about them ahead of time.

CHAPTER SIX

PEST CONTROL AND DISEASE PREVENTION

Pests and disease are the bane of many gardeners' existences. When either of these menaces get into your garden, they can leave it entirely dead in no time flat if you aren't being mindful of your maintenance and keeping an eye out for early warning signs. Unfortunately, you may still have to deal with them even when you are. The most experienced gardeners in the world still have to deal with pests and disease from time to time, they are an unlucky roll of the dice as far as the health of your plants is concerned.

If you want to keep your vegetables healthy and ensure that nothing happens to affect the way they taste, then you are going to want to be careful about how you go about treating disease or infection. Chemical insecticides can leave traces of harmful substances on your veggies that you wouldn't want to consume. There are a few ways of naturally treating these annoyances that won't harm you or your crop, but the best way to deal with them is to act in a preventative manner to stop problems before they get started.

Pest Control

An indoor vegetable garden is a lot easier to protect from pests than an outdoor one but that doesn't mean your veggies need to be doomed. There are several tricks that you can use to keep pests out of the garden and to make them regret stopping in your vegetable beds when they do. Speaking of pests, vegetable gardeners are most likely to encounter aphids, slugs, whiteflies, mealybugs, scales and spider mites. Each of these have telltale signs of infestation but mostly it comes down to the way that your plants look.

When you are out maintaining your garden, keep an eye out for discolored leaves or holes that have been chewed into them. Stems may show signs of discoloration, bruising or bumps and protrusions. These are all signs that something is in your garden that shouldn't be. If you notice any of these changes, then your next step should be to search for pests. First, use your eyes and see if you can spot any bugs roaming on your plants. Next, use a clean finger or a small rake and check through the soil around the stem of your plants to see if you can spot eggs or larvae that need to be

VEGETABLE GARDENING

removed. Finally, take a piece of tissue paper and rub the bottom side of the lower leaves. There are some pests that are too small to see with the naked eye but they will leave a piece of tissue paper bloodied and this will let you know you need to take further steps.

One of the steps you should take right away is to wash your plants. Normally you water into the soil so that the hydrogen can penetrate deep and promote root growth but washing your plants is entirely different. Use a pressurized blast of water to knock any pests free from your plants. This can greatly reduce the size of an infestation before any further treatment is needed.

VEGETABLE GARDENING

Speaking of treatment, spraying your plants with neem oil is smart both as part of a treatment and as a preventative measure. Pressed out of plants, this natural oil tastes disgusting to pests and makes them not want to chew on your plants. But it is harmless to humans and plants and so it will do no harm to your garden. Apply it weekly, regardless of whether or not you have an infestation but definitely don't skip it if you do.

You may want to release beneficial insects into your garden from time to time. Ladybugs and wasps are the two most commonly used insects for this. These beneficial bugs are natural predators of most garden pests and they will eat the pests while leaving your plants alone. Then, once there aren't enough pests left to feed them, these beneficial insects will head out into the wild to search for more food and adventure.

You can also dust your plants with flour or cinnamon, as these won't harm the plants but they will act as a deterrent to many pests and are even poisonous to others. This is especially useful if you have a problem with slugs or snails and it can be a smart idea in that case to create a line of flour around your garden to prevent these pests from even being able to enter.

If you keep an eye out for warning signs and act fast to stop infestations in their tracks, then you won't have to worry about losing your vegetables to the likes of pests.

Preventing Disease

The problem with disease is that by the time you spot it, it is too late. You might find yourself caught in a battle that takes several weeks or it can wipe out a bed overnight if it finds its way into your garden. Treating disease is rarely an option and so we need to focus our efforts on preventing it from ever getting a hold.

We've talked about it in chapter four, but you need to make sure that you get into the habit of removing dead plant matter from your garden beds. Anything that falls off your plants should be removed. This should be done on a daily basis but if this is too time consuming then you should be doing it at least as often as you water your plants. Both pests and disease will take up home in dead plant matter and use it to breed before spreading out to attack the healthy plants in the garden. Removing places where disease grows helps eliminate and prevent it in the first place.

VEGETABLE GARDENING

You should also be sanitizing your garden tools after use. You don't need to sanitize them after every cut or even after every plant but you should sanitize them at the end of the day by either washing them off or using a disinfectant cleaning solution on them. This will make sure that any harmful germs that might have been on them are killed off before the next time you use these tools. It is a good idea to kill these germs off immediately rather than give them time to fester and multiply.

We've already talked about how fertilizing your plants isn't a magic cure for all their issues and this remains true when we discuss disease. Fertilizing your plants won't magically cure them of their diseases. But properly fertilized plants are healthy plants and this is important in preventing disease. Weaker plants are more prone to infection when compared to stronger ones so consider fertilization to be a step in preventing disease.

In chapter three we talked about transplanting seedlings into our garden. When we did, the issue of black and slimy roots came up. Roots that look like this are rotting and this can spread throughout the foliage and even to other plants in the garden. Before you put a seedling into your garden, inspect it both for root rot and for signs of pests. The absolute worst experience is transplanting something new into your garden, only to find out it was diseased and now the whole bed is in danger.

Overwatering your plants is the quickest way to bring disease into your garden but even the right amount of water can be dangerous if done at the wrong time. You should only water your plants in the morning or around lunch time when the sun is the highest. Don't ever water your plants in the late afternoon, evening or night. The heat from the sun is necessary to help in watering, as it will help the water higher in the soil to evaporate. This removes moisture from around the roots, which helps to prevent root rot. Watering later in the day means there isn't as much heat to help with evaporation and so more moisture is trapped in the soil overnight and this puts your plants at risk when they really shouldn't have to be.

VEGETABLE GARDENING

Keep an eye out for signs of disease like a powdery mildew on leaves, holes, discoloration, wilting, curling leaves, leaves dropping off and more. When you understand the way a healthy plant is supposed to look, signs of disease and pests are clear as day because they stand out. Leaves turn brown instead of green, they curl up and wither when they should be stretching out and soaking up sun. When you spot problems like these, grab your shears and remove them. Prune away branches, stems, leaves and problem veggies. Quickly jumping on and removing these infected parts can save your harvest, plus eliminate a major headache before it gets really bad.

VEGETABLE GARDENING

Chapter Summary

- Pests and disease are aspects of gardening that will always find a way to show up when you least expect them to.

- An infection or infestation left unchecked will kill off even the healthiest vegetable garden.

- Dealing with disease and pests can make for major headaches, but they can both be limited by taking preventative steps.

- Outdoor vegetable gardens are at a greater risk than indoor ones, but this doesn't necessarily mean that you will personally have more problems when you garden outside. Just that you need to be more mindful of the warning signs.

- Pests like aphids, slugs, whiteflies, mealybugs, scales and spider mites are all common in vegetable gardens. Look for signs like discolored leaves with holes chewed into them. Check the soil around the stem for signs of larvae, shake the plant to see if whiteflies or other pests start scurrying around and use a piece of tissue paper to check the underside of leaves for blood trails.

- Use a blast of pressurized water to knock pests loose from your plants.

VEGETABLE GARDENING

- Apply neem oil on a weekly basis to make your vegetable plants less appealing to pests. Continue using neem oil during the treatment of an infestation.

- Beneficial insects like ladybugs and wasps will feed on pests while leaving your vegetables alone.

- Dusting plants with flour or cinnamon will create an environment that is deadly to some pests and unappealing to others, which both help prevent infestation.

- Disease can be impossible to stop once it gets into a plant, but preventing it goes a long way towards avoiding this scenario.

- Remove any dead plant matter that falls off your vegetable plants as this makes a breeding ground for pests and disease.

- Sanitize your garden tools after use to prevent germs from clinging on and multiplying before next use.

- Fertilized plants are healthier plants and so their systems are better prepared to fight off disease.

- Carefully check the roots and leaves of any plants you are transplanting into your garden ahead of time to avoid planting diseased seedlings.

VEGETABLE GARDENING

- Overwatering your plants is the quickest way to get them infected but you should also only water them before noon.

- Signs of disease like curling leaves or powdery mildew should be pruned away whenever spotted.

FINAL WORDS

As the world continues to embrace green living and sustainability practices, the number of people growing their own vegetables will keep rising. This interest is set to help the world in a lot of ways, such as by reducing the demand for chemically processed foods that ruin the environment. Another consequence of this movement will be a rise in clubs and friendships that are formed around gardening. Both of these are positive changes that you are helping to bring into the world by starting your vegetable garden.

Starting anything new is an intimidating experience for most people. As much as we enjoy surprises and trying new things, it takes effort to overcome the knowledge barrier that is needed to begin. If you just take a shovel out to your backyard and drop some seeds, you aren't going to have a very healthy garden. But by reading this book you have already proved to yourself that you are willing to seek out the knowledge you need to get gardening properly. Where other beginner's jump in too soon, you have taken the time to understand the topic and the task at hand and this is the most beneficial thing you could do for the sake of the living organisms which you are growing to provide your family with dinner.

VEGETABLE GARDENING

By this point you understand the importance of planning your garden and that it isn't just about what you want to grow but also about where you grow it and how much care you are able to realistically provide for it. You know that the soil needs to be right, that there is such a thing as too much or too little sun, and that too much water is actually a very dangerous thing. You know the importance of fertilizing your plants but also its limitations, plus what it means to be NPK balanced.

You've also learned that raising healthy vegetables is first and foremost about looking after your plants, tending to their needs and maintaining their beds. Because of this you know how to protect them from pests and how to identify when they are ready to be harvested for the biggest and tastiest yield.

All of this knowledge that you have taken the time to gather will carry you forward as a gardener and ensure that you give your plants the time and attention that they deserve. In doing so, you have guaranteed your success as a vegetable gardener and a thousand delicious meals in your future ahead.

www.ingramcontent.com/pod-product-compliance
Lightning Source LLC
Chambersburg PA
CBHW050323120526
44592CB00014B/2023